The Primordial Tradition *of* Ancient China

"Through Joscelyn Godwin's translation, we are introduced to the cornerstone of Traditionalist philosophy: Matgioi. His ideas on the Primordial Tradition are as relevant today as when they were written, with many of his writings being genuinely prophetic. Here we discover the influences of Daoism and Matgioi's understanding of it as the doctrine of heroic adepts and their transcendent force, which expands—both for themselves and others—as they participate in the "Will of Heaven" and experience the path of the Dragon in its most archaic form."

MARK STAVISH, FOUNDER AND DIRECTOR OF
THE INSTITUTE FOR HERMETIC STUDIES AND AUTHOR OF
THE PATH OF FREEMASONRY AND *EGREGORES*

The
Primordial Tradition
of Ancient China

THE ESOTERIC FOUNDATION
OF THE I CHING
AND CHINESE COSMOLOGY

MATGIOI
(Albert de Pouvourville)

Translated and Introduced by
JOSCELYN GODWIN

Inner Traditions
Rochester, Vermont

Inner Traditions
One Park Street
Rochester, Vermont 05767
www.InnerTraditions.com

Cataloging-in-Publication Data for this title is available from the Library of Congress

ISBN 979-8-88850-146-7 (print)
ISBN 979-8-88850-147-4 (ebook)

Printed and bound in China by Reliance Printing Co., Ltd.

10 9 8 7 6 5 4 3 2 1

Text design and layout by Debbie Glogover
This book was typeset in Garamond Premier Pro with Gill Sans MT Pro, Legitima
and Nobel used as display typefaces

Scan the QR code and save 25% at InnerTraditions.com.
Browse over 2,000 titles on spirituality, the occult, ancient
mysteries, new science, holistic health, and natural medicine.

Contents

Albert de Pouvourville ("Matgioi"), 1861–1939

The Masterpiece of a Warrior Metaphysician

Joscelyn Godwin

The Metaphysical Way is the first of Matgioi's many books to appear in English translation.* In one sense, it is a landmark in the West's discovery of Eastern philosophy, specifically Daoism (or Taoism). Secondly, it is a foundation stone of the modern Traditionalist current because of the crucial influence of Matgioi, and especially this work, on René Guénon. In a third sense, it contains a personal philosophy that some may find of lasting value and inspiration.

 The Metaphysical Way takes its rise from the *Yijing* (*Yiking* or *I Ching*), the ancient Chinese "Book of Changes." This is not a guide to that book, much less a manual for divination, but goes to the very basis of its conception. Matgioi concentrates on three features: the meaning of the straight versus the broken line; the first hexagram of six unbroken lines, visualized as the rise of the Dragon; and the four opening words of the ancient commentary. Legend ascribes the *Yijing* to the Chinese emperor Fuxi (Fohi or Fu Hsi), a figure so mythical

---

*Matgioi's books number between fifty and eighty, depending on how one counts the thirty volumes of *L'Héroïque aventure* (see below).

that he is sometimes pictured as having snakes for legs. Matgioi regards him as representing a school of magi or sages, unbound to any century because their wisdom is as old as humanity itself. The *Yijing* crystallizes the "Primordial Tradition," a first and truest insight into the nature of reality, from which the ancients deduced a practical philosophy applicable to all departments of life. Only in later and degenerate ages did they adapt it to the needs of the less gifted, first by inventing writing, then in the form of religions with their sacred books and institutions.

Matgioi was writing at the end of the nineteenth century for an intelligentsia disillusioned with religion, yet unsatisfied with the rank atheism and materialism that had become dogmatic in the sciences and, with Marxism, in politics. His experience in the Far East had brought him into contact with a "metaphysical way" that transcended both options. Its more immediate source was the *Daodejing* (or *Tao Te Ching*), attributed to the sage Laotseu (Lao Tzu or Laozi, fl. ca. 600 BCE), of which Matgioi made a new French version with the help of an Annamite* mandarin family. Under the dual influence of the *Yijing* and of Daoism, he then recast the primordial wisdom in modern language, resulting in the present book and its companion, *The Rational Way.*

The ancient texts have since received another century of scholarly and popular attention, and readers less interested in Matgioi's interpretation can turn to Chapter 6, where his own metaphysical insights emerge. It is these later chapters that made a lasting impression on me fifty years ago, when some footnotes in the writings of René Guénon (1886–1951) aroused my curiosity. Since Matgioi is almost unknown in the Anglosphere, either under that pseudonym or his birth name of Albert de Pouvourville, I take this opportunity to

---

*Under French protectorate and colonial rule, Annam was the general term for present-day Vietnam, and more specifically for the region between Cochinchina in the south and Tonkin in the north.

introduce his life and works, which are not without interest on their own account.

Eugène Albert Puyou, comte de Pouvourville (7 August 1861–30 December 1939) owed his surname to a district in the south of Toulouse, and his inherited title to the family's rise in the *noblesse de robe*, the high functionaries of Louis XIV's court. Guy de Pouvourville (Albert's cousin once removed) recorded what was known of his ancestry:

> I first find a fifth great-grandfather, *capitoul* [chief magistrate] of Toulouse in 1695; his son, the fourth great-grandfather, royal counselor in the presidial seat of Toulouse; then his son, the third great-grandfather, who left Toulouse and never returned. He was an officer, received the Cross of Saint Louis, and married in Landau, then in French Alsace. His son, my second great-grandfather, 1770–1851, was also an officer. He emigrated in 1791, returned in 1801, and also married in Alsace. He settled in Mulhouse, where he lived and died, not at all rich, and, like his father, having the Saint Louis Cross as his only honor. My great-grandfather was a banker in Mulhouse. Prosperity seemed to be dawning for the family, but it crashed in 1870. Two of his sons were officers, Albert's father [Théodore] and my grandfather.[1]

In 1860 Théodore de Pouvourville (1830–1921) married Alexandrine Jenny Perrotey de Jandin, and they had two children, Albert and René.[2] The sons' childhood was overshadowed by the Franco-Prussian war (1870), which left Alsace and part of Lorraine in German possession. Théodore had earned the Legion of Honor for his war service and was promoted to chief of staff of the second infantry division at Nancy, then lieutenant colonel of the 35th infantry regiment at Belfort. After the war he was instrumental in rebuilding the *Grande Couronnée*, the circuit of forts protecting Nancy, until

Maurice Barrès,   *Paul Adam,*   *Stanislas de Guaita,*
1862–1923   *1862–1920*   *1861–1897*

Albert de Pouvourville's school friends

on Bismarck's orders the forts facing the German frontier had to be demolished. Albert reminisces: "During those tragic days I was a small child of twelve, but one who from his earliest days had heard talk of war, even in the cradle; who had learned to read in the daily orders of the imperial camp of Châlons, and shot at his first pistol targets with the arms of General Saussier."[3] Théodore lived to witness the next war at first hand. In August 1914, while the Germans advanced through Lorraine, the aged colonel refused to leave Nancy for a safer haven. The fortifications held, the Germans turned their attention elsewhere, and eight months later Albert observed that the town was "perhaps the best place in France."[4]

Returning to Albert's youth, a different world opened when he entered secondary school (lycée) in Nancy and found among his classmates Maurice Barrès, Paul Adam, and Stanislas de Guaita.* Barrès (1862–1923) would become a famous novelist and politician. Adam (1862–1920) was scarcely less famous in his time as a novelist and promoter of the Symbolist movement. Guaita (1861–1897)

---

*Occasionally spelled Guaïta (with a *tréma*), as Matgioi is sometimes spelled Matgioï, though not on his own publications.

was a major figure in the esoteric movements of the fin de siècle.

Together with a couple of others, the boys formed a coterie of cultural outsiders and aspiring poets, while Guaita led the way into more arcane domains. Barrès, in his preface to Guaita's *Au seuil du mystère* (On the Threshold of the Mystery, 1915) recalls: "It is now thirty-five years since my friend and I were walking beside the Étang de Lindre under the low groves of oaks, talking of the occult sciences and problems of gnosis that beset his mind with an extraordinary force."[5]

Albert graduated from the lycée with flying colors: a double baccalaureate in science and the humanities. After a period of law studies, he entered the military academy of Saint-Cyr, breeding-ground of France's generals, graduating in 1883. His record mixes praise of his abilities with evidence for what Guy de Pouvourville calls "a scarcely credible insolence with regard to all administrations." Albert's father kept an eye on him, stationing him in his own former regiment at Nancy, from which the son repeatedly asked to be transferred. On the positive side, he was commended for his survey of the forested frontiers of Alsace, and for writing a report on the importance of the Vosges Mountains as frontier: regions that would see action in both world wars. But he was constantly in disciplinary trouble, and in April 1887 was decommissioned. On November 5 he joined the Foreign Legion as a simple soldier under a false name,[*] and in December 1887 he disembarked at Tonkin, the northern capital of French Indochina.[†]

Pouvourville's first Annamite adventure was a five-month expedition

---

[*]When asked by General Bichot, commander of the French troops, about a recent skirmish, "I finished by telling him that I am not Sergeant Tartempion, but the son of the Marquis of P., Colonel of the General Staff, former officer of ordnance under Emperor Napoleon III" (Pouvourville, *Chasseurs de pirates! . . .* , 172).
[†]Compare the biography of Ernst Jünger (1895–1998), another philosophical warrior and novelist, who skipped home at eighteen to join the French Foreign Legion and had to be brought back by his father.

up the Black River, from Hanoi almost to the Chinese frontier. Directed by Auguste Pavie (1847–1925), its purpose was pacification, surveying, and installing a primitive telegraph system. Thirty years later, when discretion was no longer necessary, Pouvourville described the dangers, diseases, and fatal accidents that beset the party in *Chasseurs de pirates!* . . . (Pirate Hunters), a narrative that rivals Joseph Conrad's novels of colonial misadventure. On his return, he found that the Legion's journal had reported him as dead: his trunks and effects had been sold, and it was difficult to get reinstated. That done, he spent the following months comfortably in Hanoi, constructing an enormous map of the sixteen *chaus* (districts) flanking the river, chatting with the Catholic Fathers, accompanying arias from Offenbach's operettas, and reflecting on his experiences.[6]

He had arrived in the protectorate equipped with an elite education and a cultural depth that put him at odds with the majority of his colleagues and even some of his superiors. He gives credit where it is due, but on the whole his verdict is damning: that beside pervasive ignorance, greed, and egotism, every administrator, on arrival, sets out to demolish what his predecessor has done, while their masters in Paris dither and argue. In contrast, the "grave mandarins . . . who have been obeying the same laws ever since their race existed, and who learn their language in the primordial books, note that we cannot keep the same ideas or follow the same measures for a year on end; that for the six years they have known us, we have gone through more changes than China has since the Great Wall was built."[7]

During the Black River expedition, Pouvourville had learned to use the colloquial language of his native company. Afterward, on meeting some of the "grave mandarins," he began the serious study of the national language and its writing: "After eighteen months of daily and continuous effort, I was able to speak quite well, with the proper accent and turns of phrase. And by the end of three years, I was writing three thousand [Chinese] characters."[8] He also wrote his first

Annamite book and had it printed in Haiphong on five-colored paper with Chinese designs woven in, and bound with string.[9] First titled *De l'autre côté du mur* (From the Other Side of the Wall), the novel described the 1883 rebellion against the French by the Black Flag rebels, from the point of view of their leader Ong Luu. In later editions it was titled *L'Annam sanglant* (Bloody Annam). It is a superbly decadent work: glamorizing the rebel as a superior and spiritual being, combining luscious description with gruesome violence, and promoting opium as the panacea for all ills.

Before his term of duty was over, and now with the rank of sublieutenant, Pouvourville applied for another year's service with the Legion, but was turned down in favor of other applicants eager for the pay and prospects of promotion. He left for France in December 1889. After a three-week stopover in Algiers, he was home by February 1890, and set to work on his first Annamite memoir, *Le Tonkin actuel 1887–1890* (Present-day Tonkin). The book opens with a colorful account of the miseries and beauties that Indochina offers, both to the French "protectors" and to its indigenous inhabitants. It continues with an account of border campaigns and a summary of financial affairs, ending with an analysis of the colony's problems and recommendations for their solution. The book was published by Albert Savine, a prolific Parisian house. According to Jean-Pierre Laurant, author of the groundbreaking 1982 monograph on Matgioi, it "shows an extraordinary spirit of independence and self-confidence, together with a remarkable knowledge of the country, both its language and its customs, considering the brevity of his stay."[10] Albert's uncle, responding to his father's concerns, advised anonymity, since the author had not asked his superiors' permission to publish. He chose the Vietnamese pen name of Mat Gioi, literally "the face of the sky/heaven." Later he would explain a triple symbolism, meaning on the physical plane, the Sun; on the intellectual plane, Great Knowledge; and on the spiritual plane, Absolute Truth.[11]

Pouvourville had fallen in love with Annam and, incidentally, with opium. This is how his lifelong habit began:

> Hoping to find a little respite [from the nightly plague of insects], I tried smoking opium: and as I found it very helpful, that is when I began the "detestable" habit of smoking every evening. Unlike many of my comrades, I was happily able to keep it within proper limits, and I never smoked more than fourteen pipes a day: a dose that, whatever the puritans say, cannot cause any physical or moral debility.*[12]

Perhaps not coincidentally, he seems to have avoided sexual indulgence of any sort, for opium, he says, is an anti-aphrodisiac. In a later book, *Le Cinquième bonheur* (The Fifth Happiness, 1911), he praises the Annamite attitude to sex as merely the means of propagating male descendants who will continue the cult of the Ancestors: "Thus, all sexuality is abolished. And to the advantage of his intelligence and inner education, the man dispenses with the passionate longings, the time wasted in love, jealousy, and all the sentimentality in which, among the Whites, woman reigns exclusively."[13]

For complicated reasons,[14] Pouvourville now applied to the colonial Civil Service, and embarked from Marseilles on August 24, 1890. After stopovers in Ceylon and Saigon, he arrived in Hanoi on October 2. Soon after, he was summoned to the Residence to learn that a "misfortune" had occurred to the indigenous Civil Guard of Sontay: brigands had killed fifty of them, and the rest of the company had vanished. Would he take over? There was little competition for such a dangerous job. To their relief, he accepted and was appointed Inspector Second Class. On October 14 he left with sole responsibility for a company of a hundred Annamite guards, all

---

*To put this in perspective, he deplores a colleague who smokes seventy-five pipes a day (Pouvourville, *Chasseurs*, 52).

"trembling like leaves," and marched to the place of the massacre. No witnesses remained, only 300 brigands who had seized the military post and cut the main road to Sontay. Pouvourville stripped the surviving posts of men to bring up his numbers, and for three months was never off his horse until the last brigand was driven off the territory at bayonet point—or worse. Their leader, Doc Huynh, was condemned to death and decapitated on June 1, 1891.

After this success, Pouvourville rested in the Catholic Mission of Sontay, often visited by his friend and master Luat (see below). "It was at this moment that I conceived the project of confronting the Truths of East and West with one another, which are really only one—and I set out the first plan of *La Voie métaphysique* [The Metaphysical Way] and the *La Voie rationnelle* [The Rational Way]."[15]

Pouvourville left Indochina again on August 5, 1891, and was home in Nancy by mid-September. This leave produced a second book for Savine, *Deux années de lutte, 1890–1891* (Two Years of Struggle): a full-length chronicle of campaigns against brigands, rebels, and other nuisances to the French administration, replete with advice on how the colony could be better managed. It is severe on the governors, on tolerance of the opium trade, and on the massive waste of money in operating a European-style army, whereas the native militias could do the job of pacification much more effectively. As one "more used to wielding the soldier's saber than the administrator's pen," Mat Gioi urges "in all frankness and without self-interest that we should be employing political and almost always pacific means, while repressive force should only be used exceptionally to make a visible and terrible example."[16] With the impassivity that marked his character, he includes sickening eye-witness descriptions of such punishments.

Pouvourville left for the Far East for the third time in January 1892,[17] and on March 17 was officially reintegrated as lieutenant in the First Foreign Regiment, stationed in Tonkin. Less is known of this tour, which may have been sponsored by the Ministry of Fine Arts.[18]

He was decommissioned on October 29 of the same year, leaving the army "under dubious conditions."

If later he exaggerated the length of his service,* it is impressive that in barely three years, alongside his military duties, he could gather so much material for his many studies of the region.

There followed three more books on colonial policy published by Savine, and one on Indochinese art.[19] The latter covers every genre from the great Cambodian temples to metalwork and lacquer, with a wealth of information on materials and techniques. It also deduces principles that accord with the Traditionalist doctrine of art, as represented later by A. K. Coomaraswamy, Titus Burckhardt, and others.[20] As Matgioi (now written as a single word) describes it, there is none of Europe's snobbish distinction between fine and applied arts, or between art and craft. Nor is any value placed on the artist's identity—he is always anonymous—and even less on originality or competition, since the truths symbolized by art are perennial.[21] For example, the human figures in Far Eastern sculpture do not represent individuals, but the higher and timeless "personality" that temporarily incarnates.[22]

While Matgioi's work up to this point had claimed authority on all things military, political, and artistic regarding Indochina, he now spoke for the cultural, spiritual, and even occult aspects of the whole Far East, or as he put it, the Yellow Races. Paying almost no attention to Buddhism, he saw Daoism as the doorway to them, and moreover let it be known that he had been initiated into a Daoist secret society. According to his book about Daoism and the Chinese secret societies, they originated in Laotseu's time (sixth century BCE), when his

---

*In the preface to *Chasseurs*, he writes (p. 7): "Thirty years ago I left [Indochina] without hope of return except for temporary missions and pleasure trips. This ended a stay of nine years, interrupted by two leaves." Advertisement in *L'Annam Sanglant*, p. 295: "Après dix ans passés en Extrême Orient . . . ." That would place him there from 1890–1898/99, which in no way agrees with other evidence.

disciples became enemies of the established order. Much later, in the seventeenth century CE, all who resisted the imperial order of the Manchu invaders "took on this glorious name."[23] Daoism served as refuge for the secret societies because it is a religion with no public rites or paid hierarchy of priests. It regards "with disdainful pity the whole dynastic, military, aristocratic, oligarchic apparatus."[24] By Matgioi's time, he says, "the mixture of disdainful mystics and the politically dissident [was] complete."[25]

Massimo Introvigne, founder of the Center for Studies on New Religions (CESNUR), confirms this ambiguous nature of Chinese (and, by extension, Annamite) secret societies, at least from the seventeenth century up to the present.[26] In their history of opposition to various oppressive powers, the societies spanned the whole range from mafialike racketeering to Masonic ritualism. Pouvourville, says Introvigne, had direct knowledge of the coexistence of politics, esotericism, and criminality within the same societies. What does that mean about his reputed initiation, and what was specifically Daoist about it?

Matgioi's scheme describes three ascending degrees within Daoism, perhaps with an eye to the three degrees of Freemasonry:[27]

> The *tongsang* teaches publicly in villages. His method is dogmatic, based on books.
>
> The *phutu* leads communities, both cloistered and wandering. He reads the same books, but with a different attitude. He is essentially contemplative. Reflection, solitude, and ecstasy give him knowledge and command of the laws of Nature.
>
> The *phap* has trained through solitary meditation but is active and errant. Completely detached from earth, he teaches through Platonic conversation adjusted to the student's level. He knows the secrets of toxicology, chiromancy, phrenology, and especially the properties of psychotropic drugs.

This classification raises several questions, such as which degree is supposed to have been conferred in Matgioi's Daoist initiation. In his novel *Le Maître des sentences* (The Master of Maxims, 1899), the title character mixes the worldly position of the *tongsang* with the methods and knowledge of the *phap*. Nor can the latter's secrets be very well guarded, since Matgioi later revealed the names and nature of the Thirteen Secret Poisons (see below). Such quibbles, however, do not detract from a novel that could not have been written without some intense and often grueling experiences. It tells of two French soldiers, friends from youth, who after many adventures and near disasters are privileged to visit the Master, Nguyen Luat. He is a physician and village chief who by strength of character and wisdom maintains a paradisal enclave, insulated from all the unrest, banditry, and oppression of the region. His younger son Thang, who acts as interpreter, has been accepted into the French brigade, and the officers are welcomed as daily partakers in refreshments and philosophic conversation, dispensed in a haze of opium smoke. One of them describes his experience: "[H]is body was inert, but his lucid spirit took flight to the summits of intelligence, which reason only attains when carried on the wings of dream."[28] Luat's teachings, however, are moral rather than metaphysical. At the end he enjoins the young men to "do good blindly and always, to repair the universal injustice in the midst of which you live; treat thanks and ingratitude with the same indifference."[29]

The novel is probably an elaboration of Pouvourville's actual relations with an influential Annamite family. On May 19, 1891, the father, Nguyen Van Luat, signed an authorization for his son Nguyen Van Cang to join the militia, and recommended him to the Frenchman's personal care. According to Guy de Pouvourville, who inherited the document and had it translated, it is in classical Chinese with interpolations in Vietnamese script.[30] Pouvourville preserved a photograph of Matgioi and Van Cang in which the officer looks formally off to

Matgioi and
Nguyen Van Cang

the side, while the smooth-faced recruit slouches comfortably with his turban, cane, and Chinese sunhat: a privileged scion of the mandarin class. He would play more than one role in Matgioi's later history.

Years later Léon Champrenaud published an account that can only have come from Matgioi himself:

Matgioi saw his master regularly, almost every evening. The latter had recognized in his pupil a mentality particularly apt for the fruitful reception of his teachings. He set out to develop unconsciously, after the Chinese method, the latent spiritual faculties that would lead to the precise understanding of the sublimity of the texts, in which, centuries before, the elements of the Yellow wisdom had been consigned as expression of the total Truth. These theoretical instructions allowed the neophyte to receive, later, the illuminative Initiation, after his affiliation with the secret societies.[31]

Whatever actually happened in Indochina, its consequences for Matgioi's esoteric career are undeniable. Jean-Pierre Laurant comments drily:

> The ambiguity of this filiation was carefully cultivated by our new Taoist: the occultist public found there the proof of a Taoist initiatic transmission; the literary public, an extraordinary adventure; the colonial administration, an example of rapport with the traditional native authorities that was indeed quite a rarity.[32]

Matgioi then settled in Paris, the center of the French occult revival. Whereas his colonial studies and novels were published by standard Parisian houses, he now turned to Edmond Bailly (1850–1916), a composer, poet, publisher, and bookseller of broadly Theosophical outlook. Beside classical texts, Bailly published translations from Helena Blavatsky and Annie Besant; poetry by André Gide, Stéphane Mallarmé, Pierre Louÿs, Henry de Régnier, and many lesser lights; bibliophile editions with Symbolist illustrations by Félicien Rops, Odilon Redon, and Maurice Denis; and musical scores by Erik Satie and Claude Debussy.[33] His bookshop near the Paris opera house hosted lectures, recitals, and sometimes séances, and anyone involved in esotericism—or merely interested in it—was liable to drop in.

Bailly's monthly journal *La Haute Science* (1893–94), a "Documentary Review of the Esoteric Tradition and Religious Symbolism," disdained the popular occultist press: witness its emblem of a siren by Félicien Rops and motto NON HIC PISCIS OMNIUM ("This isn't everybody's fish").

The first volume of *La Haute Science* contained philosophical classics and hard-to-find French works: translations from the *Zohar*,

Emblem of Edmond Bailly's publishing house

the *Bridharanyaka Upanishad*, Porphyry's *Cave of the Nymphs*, the Ethiopian Apocalypse, the Chinese text *The Invariable Middle*, Iamblichus on the Mysteries, and among later authors Frédéric Portal's *Les Couleurs symboliques* and Fabre d'Olivet's *La Cosmologie de Moïse*. The January 1894 issue presented the "Tao de Lao-Tseu: Traduction exacte par Albert de Pouvourville (Matgioi)."[34] This was a translation of the first thirty-seven paragraphs or chapters of the *Daodejing*. Later in the same year, Bailly's journal published *Le Tê de Lao-Tseu*,[35] a translation of the rest of the eighty-one chapters.* Matgioi included the following anecdote:

Having in hand the French paraphrase of Monsieur Julien, I initially had the idea of retranslating it literally into common Chinese

---

*The thirty-seven paragraphs of the *Tao* and the forty-four of the *Te* are usually united in a single work of eighty-one paragraphs: the *Daodejing* or *Tao Te Ching*.

to the doctor who was teaching me. He first smiled silently in the Oriental fashion, then became indignant and finally declared that the French must have been very hostile to the Asiatics if their scholars amused themselves by knowingly deforming the Chinese philosophers' works, and turning them into grotesque fabulations, so as to raise a laugh from the French rabble.[36]

The translation itself is peppered with remarks on the errors of Stanislas Julien (1797–1873), a philologist and linguist of the highest eminence who had published his version of the *Daodejing* in 1842. This earned a disclaimer from the editor, Léon Deschamps: "We leave to Monsieur de Pouvourville the entire responsibility for his attacks, which moreover are in no way in the spirit of *La Haute Science*."[37]

By the end of 1894, Bailly's press had issued *Le Tao de Lao-Tseu* and *Le Tê de Lao-Tseu* in limited editions of 300 copies, under a series title of *L'Esprit des races jaunes* (The Spirit of the Yellow Races). They are presented as "Translated from the Chinese by Matgioi (Albert de Pouvourville)," with a prominent note that "The *xuâtdoi* Nguyen Van Cang, Hi, younger son of the *thay-thuoc* Nguyen The Duc, Luat, Tongsang of the Rite of Laotseu, has collaborated on the translation of the Dao, for the paraphrase of the sense [*terme*] of the characters."

A collaboré
à la traduction du Tao,
pour la paraphrase du terme des caractères,
le xuâtdoï

NGUYEN VAN CANG, HI
fils puîné du thay-thuoc

NGUYEN THE DUC, LUAT,
Tongsang du Rite de Laotseu.

Nguyen Van Cang credited as collaborator

These are transparently the mandarin who figured in *Le Maître des sentences* under the very name of Luat, and his son whose military induction was enabled by Matgioi in 1891.

Matgioi's original translation has a scholarly appearance, with certain words ascribed to the oral tradition printed in brackets and italics. The problem of translating characters that denote not words but multivalent concepts is well illustrated by comparing the Matgioi–Van Cang version of a short chapter (no. 18) with the standard English translation of the same decade. One or the other has missed the whole point:

> [*Les hommes*] *qui pratiquent la Grande Voie ont la justice et l'humanité.*
> *Pratiquant l'intelligence, ils ont le respect* [*les uns des autres*].
> [*Mais*] *six hommes non unis ont l'égoïsme.*
> *L'empire troublé et confus a des officiers Hoan.**38

> When the Great Tao (Way or Method) ceased to be observed, benevolence and righteousness came into vogue.
> (Then) appeared wisdom and shrewdness, and there ensued great hypocrisy.
> When harmony no longer prevailed throughout the six kinships, filial sons found their manifestation; when the states and clans fell into disorder, loyal ministers appeared.[39]

Thirteen years later, when Matgioi included the *Daodejing* in *La Voie rationnelle* (1907), he revised it to read more smoothly and supplied notes and commentary, but the text remained substantially the

---

*Literally in English: "The men who practice the Great Way have justice and humanity. Practicing intelligence, they have respect for one another. But six men disunited have egotism. The troubled and confused empire has Hoan officers." A footnote explains that "*Hoan* is the title given to the ancient generalissimos, appointed temporarily to suppress revolts, and who were lowly regarded because of their ignorance." According to Davide Marino, *Hoan* is, in fact, a phonetic rendering of the Chinese *Hun Loan*, meaning "fall into chaos."

same. It no longer named Van Cang, but stated that "the translation has been seen and approved in the Far East by the sages who hold the heritage of Taoist Science, and the son of one of them, who came to France for this very purpose, has collaborated up to the last day on our translation and on the commentaries and notes that follow it."[40] However, modern linguists perceive "gross errors" concerning the Chinese characters, precluding any idea of transmission within a formal organization. After mentioning this, Jean-Pierre Laurant summarizes: "Apparently, Matgioi, who had an elementary knowledge of classical Chinese, had had an unpunctuated Chinese text read by someone who did not understand it very well, but knew the Confucian commentaries and embroidered and glossed the whole thing."[41] Matgioi's effort therefore takes its place in the reception history of the *Daodejing*, showing how it was understood and explicated by the learned classes of nineteenth-century Annam, then given to a Francophone public avid for Eastern wisdom.

La Haute Science ceased publication after its second year (1894), having proved too highbrow to retain subscribers. Matgioi turned to the longstanding journal *L'Initiation*, run by Stanislas de Guaita's friend Papus (Dr. Gérard Encausse, 1865–1916). From June 1894 to January 1895, under the pseudonym of "MoGd," Matgioi expounded "The Seven Elements of Man and Chinese Pathogeny,"[42] illustrating with eleven hand-drawn diagrams how different conditions such as sleep, cholera, epilepsy, or death affect the material, psychic, and spiritual elements that make up the human being.

These, too, were collected in book form and joined the series of *L'Esprit des races jaunes*, whose other volumes were on "Opium: Its Practical Use," "Quandzgu's Treatise on Errant Influences," and "Taoism and the Chinese Secret Societies."[43]

The treatise on opium argues for the safety and benefits of its use, and that it is far less tiring and depressive than ether, absinthe, or alcohol. However, the smoker must be practical, intelligent, and aware that opium offers three possible effects: soporific (also called hedonistic),

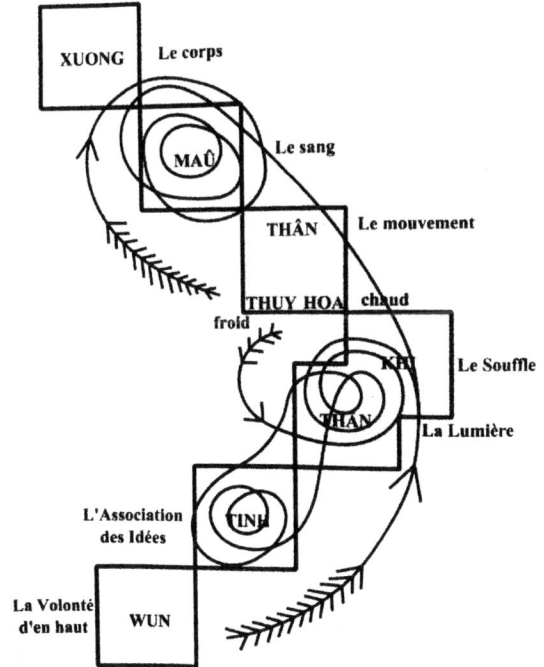

The Seven Elements of Man, in the condition of normal life. Translation of French terms, reading down: Body, Blood, Movement, hot, cold, Breath, Light, Association of Ideas, Higher Will.

excitant, or toxic. He must choose which he desires—usually the first—and ensure that the opium is correspondingly prepared. Each effect is caused by a different blend of alkaloids, which Matgioi analyzes in chemical terms. The first effect requires boiling the opium in alcohol to eliminate the papaverine and the thebaine. The residue contains only morphine and perhaps codeine (irrelevant to the hedonist). Taken thus, Matgioi assures us, opium is an absolute protection against cholera, dysentery, sunstroke, hunger, thirst, and much more: in short, "truly a celestial gift."[44]

Quangdzu's treatise on "errant influences" belongs to the exoteric side of Daoism, being a Dantesque description of the after-death state, full of punishments, demons, and rebirths as pigs or buffalo. Like its Christian and Muslim counterparts, it seems intended to scare believers into good behavior. Van Cang is again credited with helping Matgioi translate it from the Chinese, but the many questioning footnotes show that neither found it an easy task. Matgioi excuses it by explaining that this apparent hell is, in reality, "the point of time and space in which individuals after earthly death undergo the modifications necessary for their entry into another personal and responsible life."[45]

By the century's end, Matgioi was entering respectable middle age. In 1895 he had married Marthe Garnier de la Villesbret (died 1914) and fathered a daughter (Andrée-Marthe, died 1926).[46] Apparently, this did not greatly affect his lifestyle, for, according to Laurant, "the marriage was unhappy and the couple soon separated, though without divorcing," Marthe going to live with her mother.[47] His expertise on colonial matters gave him entrance and employment in the establishment circles that he had earlier despised. In 1898 he joined the Institut Colonial Français, and in 1904 began a tenure of many years as Secretary General of the Comité des Congrès Coloniaux (Committee of Colonial Congresses). Tunisia honored him with the Order of Glory (Nichan Iftikhar), Liberia with the Order of African Redemption, and France with the Legion of Honor as Chevalier (1920) and Officier (1932).[48] Guy de Pouvourville surmises that he also worked for the intelligence services.[49]

Guaita in the meantime had become a celebrated authority on occult philosophy, especially its darker side. In 1888 he had founded the Ordre Kabbalistique de la Rose-Croix on a basis of Christian Kabbalah, Rosicrucian principles, and Hermetic philosophy. The order simulated a university, directing courses of study and conferring degrees up to the doctorate. While neither the academic nor the Christian aspect appealed to Matgioi, the three-way friendship with Barrès and Guaita flourished,* and Matgioi was much affected by the latter's death on December 19, 1897, at the age of thirty-six. In later tributes Matgioi fulminates against the Guaita family, bigoted Catholics embarrassed by Stanislas's reputation, who deliberately dispersed his magnificent

---

*Barrès acted as second in Guaita's challenge of Jules Bois and Joris-Karl Huysmans to a duel, which was resolved through apologies. See Guaita's account in *L'Initiation* 18/5 (Feb. 1893): 182–88.

library in order to deprive occultists of access to it, and denied that any of his notes, personal documents, or letters survived.*

During the seven years from 1898 to 1904, Matgioi published only fiction, poetry, works on the Far East, studies of colonial problems, and a plan for the reform of Saint-Cyr, his old academy. He returned to the esoteric scene in April 1904, with a new journal directed and presumably financed by himself. It was titled *La Voie* (The Way), being the French equivalent of *Dao*.[50] The monthly numbers included articles, poems, book reviews, reports on relevant events in France and elsewhere, advertisements for new and rare books, and even a financial bulletin with investment tips by one J. Dargent.† Since Matgioi was the editor and proprietor, no one could object to a certain "Albert Puyoo" contributing his own poems, called *Rimes Jacobines*. There was also a social dimension: from December 1904, subscribers were invited on the second Thursday of every month to dine at 7:30 at the Restaurant Voltaire, Place de l'Odéon, at the price of four francs *tout compris*.

La Voie had a regular section of "Correspondence from the Far East," signed by none other than Nguyen Van Cang, the son of Matgioi's Taoist master and soldier in his militia. That much is documented, but the communications are blatantly spurious. Most are about Tibet, rather than Annam, and, as Davide Marino's research has shown, they parrot information—and misinformation—from the travels of Abbé Huc (1844–46), H. P. Blavatsky's *Secret Doctrine* (1888), and Nicholas Notovich's *La Vie inconnue de Jésus-Christ* (1894). Marino concludes that Van Cang was merely serving as an alias for Matgioi's own invention.‡[51] In all probability this included his purported visit to

---

*According to Les Amis de Guaita, "Guaita et la Problème du mal," *La Voie* (April 1906): 1–13, and Matgioi, *Stanislas de Guaita* (Librairie Hermétique, 1907), Guaita sent hundreds of pages of correspondence to the Far East—presumably to Matgioi.

†A pun on *J'ai d'argent*—"I've got money."

‡Pouvourville maintained the fiction by using "Nguyen-Te-Duc-Luat" as the purported author of *Physique et psychique de l'opium* (Les Éditions du Monde Moderne, 1925), while signing the introduction with his own name.

France mentioned in *La Voie rationnelle*. He took on a different guise in Pouvourville's late book on the Annamite mentality* as a chief's son named Nguyen, who, after serving eight years in the Annamite militia, spends six months as Matgioi's guest.[52] In this lively narrative, Nguyen lands in Marseilles and takes the express train to Paris. When it enters a tunnel, he is sure that his last hour has come. He is thrilled to be lodged in a little room next to his master's library, for he has a great reverence for books. Matgioi has taught him the alphabet, but Nguyen is not impressed by the French having only twenty-four letters, whereas the Annamites have 917 "keys" and 108,000 characters! They visit all the sights, the libraries, the Sorbonne and the Latin Quarter, the racing resort of Longchamps, and pay their respects to Matgioi's mother in the family home, "a sort of fortified manor house [*maison forte*], converted into a hunting lodge [*tournebride de chasse*]."[53]

Nguyen reacts to it all with naive astonishment, shocked to see his former commander waiting in line at the bank or post office, and obeying policemen when crossing a street. There is no suggestion of literary collaboration. At best there is a *Persian Letters* flavor,[54] as the host gets a fresh perspective on his own milieu.

A visit from a mature Nguyen Van Cang, his name prominent in at least three of Matgioi's books, should have made waves in the small world of Parisian occultism. Surely, he would have been paraded around, lionized at Bailly's bookshop, begged for initiations. There is none of this in Matgioi's charming but childish guest, nor a breath of external evidence of such an interesting visitor. Nonetheless, the seed was planted for the rumor of a Daoist initiate who had given oral teaching to Guénon, which became standard Guénonian lore.[55]

The leading articles in each number of *La Voie* were by Matgioi himself. From April to December 1904, they comprised the nine chapters of the present work. Its publication in book form was announced

---

*This book, *L'Annamite* (1932), appeared in an instructional series called *Comme ils pensent* (How They Think).

Cover illustration of Matgioi's series "Bibliothèque de La Voie"

the following summer, when *La Voie métaphysique* appeared from the Société d'Éditions Contemporaines in the series "Bibliothèque de La Voie." The cover illustration, signed with the unattributed monogram NG or GN, pictures a Sphinx before the rising sun with sacred ibises, a floral frieze, and, as the only Daoist feature, the Taiki symbol. The work is dedicated "To my masters: This book, in which I have put all the thoughts that they have given me."

By this time the companion work, *La Voie rationnelle*, was already appearing in parts. It ran from March 1905 with "Laotseu" and ended in February 1907 with "Le Taoïsme Contemporain." This was not a coherent and original treatise like *La Voie métaphysique*, but a gathering of Matgioi's previous translations and studies including the *Daodejing*, the short text *Kan-ing* ("Treatise on Actions and Their Retributions"), some of the *Esprit des races jaunes* pieces, and a chapter on toxicology describing how to make thirteen "secret" poisons and, obligingly, their antidotes. Publication of *La Voie rationnelle* in book form followed in May 1907, its cover design uniform with its predecessor, after which *La Voie* ceased.[56] A companion volume on the teachings of Confucius, to be called *La Voie sociale*, was promised to complete the trilogy, but never appeared.*

La Voie rationnelle carried a commendatory Preface signed "Alta," who thanks "my dear Matgioi for showing us the unity of plan and action in the world of the spirit; in the universal religious work, the unity of the true catholicism, of the religion that binds the spirit [or mind] and the heart across all differences, all men from all nations and all epochs." This alludes to a new phase of Matgioi's activity and orientation, for Alta was the Abbé Calixte Mélinge (1842–1933), a Roman Catholic priest, and by this time Matgioi himself was a bishop, no less.

That requires some explanation. Matgioi's consecration was in the Nouvelle Église Gnostique Universelle (New Universal Gnostic Church), founded by Jules-Benoît Doinel in 1889 or early 1890 after a séance at the Countess of Caithness's residence, in which the spirit of a medieval Cathar bishop—or else one of the divine Aeons[57]—had manifested and urged a revival of the Gnostic Church. Its principle was "to represent and restore the ancient Christian Church, democratic and egalitarian."[58] Matgioi may have joined it shortly after his return from Indochina, for he was present at the synod of 1893, along with his future collaborators Léon Champrenaud (1870–1925) and Léonce Fabre des Essarts (1848–1917).[59] The church itself was small and elitist. Its members (almost all of them bishops) extended its tentacles into the various Masonic, Martinist, and Rosicrucian orders, the Theosophical Society, and its would-be rival, the Hermetic Brotherhood of Luxor.

---

*Part of it may have been used in Matgioi's *L'Annamite*, which begins with a lengthy explanation of Confucianism.

By 1895 the primacy had passed to Fabre des Essarts, whose title was "Synésius, Patriarch of the Gnostic Church of France." Léon Champrenaud was "Théophane, Bishop of Versailles" and Matgioi, "Simon, Bishop of Tyre and the Orient."*

A decade later, *La Voie*, besides being the organ for Matgioi's own Daoist-inspired writings, also served as such for the Gnostic Church. The March 1905 number of the journal promised its subscribers a "complete treatise of modern Gnosticism," which began in April with "Les Ténèbres extérieures" (The Outer Darkness) and ended in September 1906 with "L'Étoile flamboyante" (The Blazing Star). The articles were signed "Simon-Théophane," later clarified as a collaboration of Matgioi and Champrenaud. Just as with Matgioi's *Voies*, the Gnostic series was then issued in book form (1907) with the title *Les Enseignements secrets de la Gnose* (The Secret Teachings of Gnosis), prefaced by Fabre des Essarts, who writes:

> You, my very dear and valiant Cooperators, with an apostolic zeal that fills my whole soul with a sweet joy, have re-immersed our beloved Gnosis in the Oriental springs, which are its true origin, and thus completed Valentinus with Wen-Wang, and commented on the divine mysteries of the TAU with the sacred teachings of the TAO.[60]

These sugary endorsements by an abbé and a patriarch agree less with Matgioi's own style than with the triple status he now enjoyed as man of letters, initiate into Far Eastern wisdom, and frequenter of the corridors of secular power. They also served his own program of accommodating to modern needs a "traditional" body of cosmogonic and metaphysical knowledge, whose traces were as evident to him in ancient Gnosticism as in Daoism, though he made no attempt at a

---

*After Simon Magus, the first-century magician and Gnostic.

scholarly engagement with the former. The Gnostic essays propound the same philosophy as in *La Voie métaphysique* under scarcely different terms, including Being and Nonbeing, Universal Possibility, nature of the Demiurge, equivalence of death and birth, contrast of primordial Tradition with revealed religions, and so forth, and with the same intention of offering "a practical doctrine, in the sense that it seeks to influence men and guide them, through multiple transformations, toward what it knows to be their final and excellent end."[61]

A frequent contributor to *La Voie* was Francis Warrain (1867–1940), a sculptor, collector, mathematician, and author of books on Kabbalah, Johannes Kepler, Hoëne Wronski, and Charles Henry. Matgioi wrote in a preface to Warrain's philosophical testament, *La synthèse concrète* (1910):

> Three years ago, a few men joined in a group under the same impulse, the same ardor, and the same open-mindedness. Occult philosophy, which is the true High Science, was the sole object of their affection, the sole goal of their researches. They remained united in the spiritual community of their labors and aspirations. From their patient and fruitful investigations there grew and developed works which, given to the public, rejoiced the very small number of dispassionate thinkers, whom the turmoil of this century has not laid low.[62]

This implies that the group formed in 1907, when *La Voie* ceased publication with the May number. It was probably the little-documented "Groupe Paléosophique," a group of open-minded researchers into lost wisdom, which beside Warrain included Oswald Wirth, Ernest Britt, Pierre Piobb, Eugène Caslant, and Alexandre Rouhier.[63] Each had a visible career on the borderlines of esotericism with other disciplines. Wirth (1860–1943) had been Guaita's friend and secretary, and was an authority on the Tarot. Britt (1857–after 1950) was a composer and music theorist, later married to the American heiress Mary Shillito, who financed the esoteric publishing house of Véga. Piobb (1874–1942) wrote on Nostradamus, astrology, and translated Robert Fludd on geomancy. Colonel Caslant (1865–1940) wrote on geomancy, music theory, and psychical research. Rouhier (1875–1968) was an authority on peyote and other entheogens, managed Éditions Véga, and is sometimes identified as author of *L'Architecture naturelle*, a monumental book published by that house in 1949.[64] For Matgioi, this nonreligious group offered an alternative to the squabbles within the Gnostic Church and attempts to give it a more Christian orientation.[65]

Matgioi's collection of essays *Le Cinquième bonheur* (The Fifth Pleasure, 1911) shows a more *mondain* milieu. Each essay carries a different dedicatee, including Maurice Barrès, Judith Gautier (1845–1917), Camille Saint-Saëns (1835–1921), Pierre Loti (1850–1923), General Oscar de Négrier (1839–1913) of the 1885–86 Tonkin campaign, Madame Paul Deschanel (wife of the future president of France), princesses Radolin and Galitzin, and fellow writers on oriental themes.

After the publication in 1907 of *La Voie rationnelle* and *Les Enseignements secrets de la Gnose*, Matgioi's fertile pen produced no more metaphysical works, but continued to draw on his early experiences in the Far East. It is possible that he returned there for one or more "temporary missions." In November 1909, writing as "Albert comte de Pouvourville," he completed a study of opium and alcohol in Indochina, summarized as a lecture at the École des Hautes Études Commerciales and published in full in January 1910.[66] It treats social, medical, commercial, and political aspects, quoting official documents and statistics gathered as lately as the previous July, and shows the obstacles to every attempt, however well-intentioned, to manage a culture utterly different from Republican France. For instance, when the Annamite mandarin class was induced to set a good example by publicly renouncing opium-smoking, they surprised the colonial medics by showing no withdrawal symptoms. It turned out that they were taking morphine tablets as a supposed "cure." Since opium poppies were not raised in Indochina, their products came across the long frontiers with China and (British) India, making it impossible to control traffic, whether legal or otherwise, or profitably tax it. China exercised much looser controls in both fields, while its alcohol contained percentages of toxins far exceeding French standards. Pouvourville's impartial and professional report is interesting in view of his lifelong use of the drug, and his rare ability to master it.

Early in 1908 there occurred an echo of the foundation of the Universal Gnostic Church in 1889, at the behest of a medieval Cathar's spirit.[67] This time it was a group of Martinists who were holding séances in the Rue des Canettes near the church of Saint-Sulpice, at which the communicating spirits included Adam Weishaupt (founder of the Illuminati of Bavaria); Cagliostro; Frederick the Great; and Jacques de Molay, last Grand Master of the Knights Templar. The latter decreed that the Order of the Temple be refounded, and commanded the participants to go to the apartment of René Guénon on the Île Saint-Louis, and install him as head of an "Ordre du Temple Rénové." Guénon, an ex-philosophy student, was in Paris investigating and joining every possible esoteric, occultist, or Masonic group, and he consented. His presence at the order's first séance on March 6, 1908, resulted in a flood of information that must have astonished the company. Under forty-five headings, it included titles of many of Guénon's future articles and books, including *The Multiple States of the Being* and *The Symbolism of the Cross*. Other topics came from the works of Saint-Yves d'Alveydre and of Matgioi himself (e.g., No. 44, "helicoidal representation of the cycles").[68] Presumably, the "spirits" were projections of Guénon's own mind, but that does not lessen one's awe at what this twenty-one-year-old mind contained.

In June 1908, Guénon worked as a secretary for the Spiritualist and Masonic Congress, convened by Papus, where he met Fabre des Essarts and perhaps Champrenaud and Matgioi. He joined their Gnostic Church and was consecrated Bishop of Alexandria under the name of

Palingénius ("reborn," a play on *René*). That summer saw a breakup between Papus and the neo-Gnostics and the latters' expulsion from the Martinist Order, with Guénon coming down, for the time being, on their side.[69] The next year, 1909, Fabre des Essarts and Guénon launched a monthly journal suitably titled *La Gnose*. The cover illustration, reminiscent of Matgioi's *Voies* but devoid of Daoist imagery, combines Egyptian themes (sphinx, pyramids, obelisk, ankh) with the apocalyptic Lamb and Book of Seven Seals, the Four Rivers of the Earthly Paradise, and the Gnostic Tau cross. There are also a swastika (for Buddhism), intersecting triangles (for Kabbalah), and a head of Athena and her olive branches. This assemblage must have displeased the editor, for in the second year the cover simply boasted an inscription for adepts in Sanskrit, Hebrew, Chinese, and Arabic to decipher.

La Gnose opened with Guénon's first doctrinal article, "The Demiurge": an argument for the ultimate unreality of evil (and,

Cover of René Guénon's journal
La Gnose *(1909–12)*

consequently, of good as well) and a remarkable achievement, sketching the metaphysical system that was the basis for Guénon's entire oeuvre.[70] Later articles treated topics already adumbrated in the New Templars' séances, especially high-grade Freemasonry, metaphysical mathematics, and a large part of his future book *Le Symbolisme de la croix.* Their germ, however, was already present in the neo-Gnostic teachings, from which Guénon drew many of his principles without actually quoting them verbatim.[71] And those teachings reformulated concepts that Matgioi had published in the present work.

Chains of transmission apart, traditional metaphysics is no one's property. From Fuxi onward, each exponent has couched it in terms appropriate to time, place, and audience. In *La Voie* of 1904, Matgioi had introduced the language of Daoism and the *Yijing.* During 1905 *Les Enseignements secrets de la Gnose* had included concepts from Gnosticism, such as the Demiurge, and from Kabbalah, such as Adam Kadmon, the universal man. In 1908 Guénon's evident familiarity with this literature had erupted in the séances of the new Templars. In the meantime, he had discovered the nondualist Vedanta of Shankaracharya (eighth century) and was able to supplement the language of his Gnostic colleagues with long quotations from the Indian sage.*

La Gnose had an even shorter life than *La Voie,* from November 1909 to February 1912. Matgioi contributed only one brief but pungent article, on "The Metaphysical Error of Sentimentally Based Religions,"[72] in which he concludes that "Love being the most natural, the most ardent, the least purified of passions, to love God is nonsense—and if it were not nonsense, it would be an insult." Under Guénon's rule, Warrain and the Groupe Paléosophique were conspicuously absent. Nor

---

*Although Guénon may have known enough Sanskrit to consult Shankara's original, his quotations read like reworkings of the French translation by Félix Nève, *Atmabodha ou de la connaissance de l'esprit* (Imprimérie Impériale, 1866). When Guénon quoted the Daoist writings, even when citing Matgioi, he used the academically respected translations of Léon Wieger, S.J., for example, *Taoïsme* (Guilmoto, 1911–1913).

was there any more talk of Templars: Guénon had been instructed (by the spirits?) to dissolve the new Templar order in 1911, and he probably abandoned the Gnostic Church at the same time.[73] Two other preoccupations were evident. First, *La Gnose* published the *Archéomètre*, the great posthumous work of Saint-Yves d'Alveydre (1842–1909), to the annoyance of Papus and the "Amis de Saint-Yves" who were preparing a far more elegant presentation.[74] Guénon would never quite abandon his fidelity to certain of Saint-Yves' notions, like the King of the World and his underground realm of Agarttha.[75] Second, there were several contributions on Islamic esotericism by "Abdul-Hâdi," pen name of Ivan Aguéli (1869–1917), a Swedish painter who had been initiated in Egypt into a Sufi order.[76] Together with Matgioi on Daoism, Guénon on Vedanta, and a Gnostic approach to Christianity, the foundations were being laid for what Theosophists had been propounding for thirty years: a transcendent unity beyond the diversity of religions, rooted in the unfathomed past. But whereas Matgioi, like Blavatsky, regarded the revealed religions as lowly forms of Tradition adapted to the "gross and infantile brains" of later humanity,[77] Guénon would respect them as transparent gateways to esoteric truth.

Aguéli transmitted his Sufi initiation to Guénon and Champrenaud, who took the respective names of Abd al-Wahid and Abd al-Haq. Matgioi also added to Guénon's collection of initiations with induction into his Daoist "secret" society.[78] How seriously one regards these initiations depends on one's view of what actually occurs in them, and whether (as Guénon would maintain) they have a permanent effect on the psychic or spiritual state of the recipient. The same applies to Freemasonry, many of whose initiates believe no such thing. Nor did these initiations entail conversion, much less practice of the religions from which they emanated. The problem hardly arises in the case of Gnosticism, an extinct religion that could be reinvented at will. But Sedgwick, discussing Aguéli, writes that "The Sufi path, it is stressed, is a path *within* Islam: the scrupulous practice of mainstream Islam is a precondition for access to the *batin*" (the esoteric dimension of the faith).[79] Daoism, too, while not a formal religion, does entail a series of ritual practices and rules for the conduct of life.

When Matgioi came to write in retrospect about his Daoist initiation, he gave a view of the matter free from mystery-mongering and pretension, while acknowledging its life-changing impact:

> This initiation was only bestowed on me after twelve months of persistent and even thankless labor. Far from being an unveiling of the Asiatic mysteries, it was only an invitation to a work that I pursued for the nine [sic] years that I spent in Indochina, in various situations. Beside certain incidental but still valuable notions, I mainly acquired the certitude of my imperfection, my ignorance, and my unworthiness. This, it seems, is the first step of wisdom. I greatly fear that I have not risen to others. But this poor ascent has nevertheless been extremely useful in my existence: it has given me defiance of the ego, and disdain for the universe.[80]

Matgioi's publications continued with poems, comments on Indochinese matters, a re-edition of *De l'autre côté du mur* as *L'Annam sanglant* (Bloody Annam), prefaces to others' works, and another book on opium.[81] Then came the First World War, whose impact on Lorraine and Alsace he witnessed at first hand. In *Les Terres meurtries* (The Wounded Lands), published in 1915, he shows knowledge of every inch of the territory, together with its past history, topography, geology, fauna and flora. All this gives a deep and tragic background to the waste of lives and land but, as mentioned above, the book ended on a hopeful note. The sequel, *Jusqu'au Rhin: Les Terres promises* (To the Rhine: The Promised Lands, 1916) includes the first book, then continues in similar style to describe Alsace, with its cities of Mulhouse, Colmar, and Strasbourg. Albert's father lived to see them returned to France at the Armistice.

Matgioi's wartime writing was published under his birth name, as was the lighter fiction published after the war. *L'Homme que a mis les Boches dedans* (1919, roughly translatable as "The Man Who Fooled the Krauts") is set in the prewar years. Its hero, Jacques Aubain, joins the intelligence services after graduating from Saint-Cyr. He is a master of languages, disguises, high social contacts, and survival skills, which he uses for spying on the Germans, discovering weak points in their preparations for the inevitable conflict. Each of the six chapters is a separate tale, with the suspense, local color, caricature, and warrior ethic that one expects of the genre; but the ending is grim, when Aubain finds that his fiancée has been raped and murdered. Guy de Pouvourville suspected that the stories were partly autobiographical but could never discover from his uncle what was so, and what was invented, either there or in the Far Eastern novels.[82]

He gave Jean-Pierre Laurant this impression of Matgioi's personality in the 1920s:

As a child I saw him twice, a little after the Great War. I was probably seven or eight, and he in his well-preserved sixties. He was very elegant: not tall but slim, very upright, his face thin and already parchmentlike, his nose fine and aquiline, light eyes sunk deep in their monocled orbits: he had the aspect of a lord—but a secretive one. I was taken to him the second time because he was my legal guardian. I can still hear the sound of the many locks and of the grille that the valet drew aside before opening the door of the apartment in Passy, where he lived with his father. He was cautious, and with good reason: one of his secrets could be guessed by the smell of opium, which I did not recognize at the time, but which grabbed the visitor who entered between the large, solemn, and fine furnishings. Was that his only secret? We will speak of it later.

At the time he had the reputation in the rest of the family of being a difficult man, and one seldom saw him. He had sifted his family relations, apparently only keeping those who had surrounded his childhood and youth, especially on his mother's side. On my side he only liked my father, who had been killed in 1914. Besides, he had separated from his wife, and we always saw her side, which may have displeased him. But he remained as a presence in my childhood mind, with a sort of legend, a special aura.[83]

By the time that Guy de Pouvourville renewed relations with his uncle, around 1930, Matgioi had quietly remarried and was living in Châtenay,* in a "large plain house backed by a long sloping garden where he never set foot."[84] While his first wife is faintly documented in the records of the French aristocracy, we know next to nothing about his second, Marguerite Jeanne Ménard (1893–1951). At a literary banquet in 1929 she was presented as the Marquise de Pouvourville,[85] so evidently Albert had assumed the title of marquis on the death of his father, though he only flaunted it on special occasions. When Guy visited the couple, Madame de P. annoyed him with her constant chatter. Life cannot have been easy for her, either. The marriage was childless, and she survived the Second World War "if not in destitution, at least in difficulties—which was hardly exceptional at the time."[86] Upon her death, all that passed to Guy were some family mementos. Of Matgioi's own correspondence, like Guaita's, there was no trace, though rare examples of his writing may be of interest to the graphologist.[87]

The First World War had extinguished the French occult revival, both in fact and symbolically with the death of Papus in 1916, from tuberculosis caught while doctoring the wounded. The chief survivors of fin-de-siècle occultism were Theosophy and Spiritualism. By 1920 several offshoots of Blavatsky's movement were flourishing, notably Annie Besant and Charles W. Leadbeater's proclamation of Jiddu Krishnamurti as the World Teacher, and Rudolf Steiner's Anthroposophy. Spiritualism took on new vigor from attempts to

---

*Of the several Châtenays in France, I presume this was Châtenay-Malabry, a southwestern suburb of Paris.

*Letter from Matgioi to his friend Jean Ajalbert (1863–1947),
Director of the Manufacture Nationale de Tapisseries, Beauvais*

communicate with those fallen in the war. René Guénon (a noncombatant on grounds of health) was disgusted by all of this. He resumed university studies at the Sorbonne, culminating in a doctoral thesis on Hindu doctrines. His hopes for an academic position were dashed when the thesis was rejected, with the pointed remark that "he is all too ready to believe in a mystical transmission of a truth that first appeared to the human race in the first ages of the world."[88] Permanently embittered against the Academy, Guénon also drew on his prewar experiences to demolish Theosophy and Spiritualism.[89] These polemical but entertaining volumes, together with an augmented version of his thesis,[90] were Guénon's first book-length publications, preparing the way for a purified Traditionalism.

Matgioi, too, had completed his vision of a Primordial Tradition in the prehistoric past that had ramified worldwide, and still shone through the variety of its progeny. In a commendatory preface to a 1926 book by Madame Blavatsky (in itself, a snub to Guénon), *Au pays des montagnes bleues*,* he writes a breathless paragraph that embraces primitive Chinese religion; Daoism; the legend that Jesus' lost years took him to the Orient; Mesopotamian religion and science; the religion of Egypt; Zoroastrianism; Hinduism (summed up in the single name of Ram); the oracular origins of Greco-Roman paganism; Tibetan Bön and Buddhism; the gift to Europe of esoteric Christianity, itself derived from Mahayana Buddhism; Kabbalah; and, lastly, the futility of exoteric religions that worship Blavatsky's *bête noire*, the Personal God. Perhaps that is why Islam and even the Sufis do not make the list.

> Whether through the trigrams that Fohi saw on the scales of the Dragon emerging from the waters; the ideographic characters that

---

*H. P. Blavatsky, *Au pays des montagnes bleues* (Editions du Monde Moderne, 1926). The book, first published in Russian, was an account of the discovery of the Nilgiri Mountains and their inhabitants. It appeared in English as *The People of the Blue Mountains* (Theosophical Press, 1930).

Laotseu entrusted to the Guardians of the Western Gate, before going to die in the region where Jesus worked during his secret life; the cuneiforms that the Magi of Assur inscribed on stone beneath the wings of the sacred Bulls; the hieroglyphs that the high priests of Sesostris and Ramses chiseled on the stelae, pyramids, and obelisks of Egypt; the propositions of Zoroaster and the worshipers of the Celestial Fire; the traditions of Ram, or the oracles of Delphi; the Lamaist sources from which the Essenes tried to refresh the thirsty Aryan; the mysterious tablets fallen from Sinai; or the desperate appeals rising from Babel to the inert and deaf Heavens—the truth is one, knowledge is one. It is only the protean and incomplete spirit of the generations that would find different words, divergent philosophies, and adversarial rites for the expression and representation of the One Thing.[91]

To sum it up in Matgioi's oft-quoted dictum: "Love Religion—mistrust religions."[92]

In March 1930, Guénon left for Egypt in the company of Mary Shillito (see above), with the purported object of collecting Sufi materials for Véga, a new publishing house that she was financing.[93] Something occurred between them that sent her back to Europe, leaving him stranded in Cairo and almost without resources, but with qualifications that opened the doors of the Sufi community. He never left the country again. Before dropping him from its list, Véga published his two most metaphysical works, *Le Symbolisme de la croix* (1931) and *Les États multiples de l'Être* (1932). Both cite *La Voie métaphysique* and adopt Matgioi's technique of explaining metaphysical matters by imagining geometric figures. This however was a long-distance acknowledgment, not a sign of friendship. The two had very little in common on the personal level and had long gone their own ways.

In 1932, the adventures of Jacques Aubain (*L'Homme qui a mis les Boches dedans*) were reprinted as *A-29 agent secret*, followed the next year by a sequel, *Nouveaux avatars d'A-29*. A listing in the latter gives the measure of Matgioi/Pouvourville's literary success in terms of sales: *L'Annam sanglant*, easily his bestseller, had reached 45,000 copies; *Le cinquième bonheur*, 3,000; *L'Heure silencieux*, 20,000; *Jusqu'au Rhin*, 7,000; *Le Mal d'argent*, 5,000; *A-29, agent secret*, 25,000; *Louis-Gabriel, pirate*, 8,000; and *Griffes rouges sur l'Asie*, 5,000. This stream soon became a torrent. The septuagenarian novelist, writing as "Albert de Pouvourville, de l'Institut Colonial," had found his final métier in the genre of military anticipation. The torrent comprised thirty books under the general title *L'Héroïque aventure* (1934–35). They appeared "Each Thursday, ninety-six illustrated pages, three hours of the most gripping reading,"[94] and were reissued in six stout volumes. By this time there was no doubt that Hitler's Germany was preparing for war, and that it would be fought with new and fearsome weapons. The lurid covers and illustrations by the prolific illustrator Louis-Félix Claudel (1895–1948) show ray guns, "navigyres," "aquatanks," and other fantasies of art-deco science fiction.

For the sake of documentation not found elsewhere, here are the titles, from which one can guess the main lines of the plot:

LA GUERRE PROCHAINE (The Forthcoming War)
I. *Les Navigyres* (The Navigyres), comprising: 1. *Les Navigyres*; 2. *Alerte sur Paris* (Alert over Paris); 3. *Le Mur de lumière* (The Wall of Light); 4. *La Route de feu* (The Fiery Path); 5. *Paris l'invincible* (Paris the Invincible).

L'HÉROÏQUE AVENTURE (The Heroic Adventure)
II. *Batailles aériennes* (Air Battles), comprising: 1. *Le Frontier d'acier* (The Steel Frontier); 2. *Les Canons-longs* (The Long Cannons); 3. *Au secours de Prague* (To the Rescue of Prague); 4. *Alpinistes et sous-marins* (Alpinists and Submarines); 5. *Les Aquatanks* (The Floating Tanks).

The navigyre destroys a
Nazi plane (cover illustration
by Louis-Félix Claudel)

"The zenithoscope: a
recently perfected device"
(L'Héroïque Aventure, I:61)

III. *Fortresses mouvantes* (Mobile Fortresses), comprising: 6. *Les Crimes de la science* (The Crimes of Science); 7. *Nos savants repliquent* (Our Scientists Respond); 8. *La Marche vers Stuttgart* (The March to Stuttgart); 9. *Prise de Karlsruhe* (Karlsruhe Taken); 10. *Croiseurs et torpilles* (Cruisers and Torpedos).

IV. *Le Rayon orange* (The Orange Ray), comprising: 11. *L'Europe en armes* (Europe up in Arms); 12. *Tirs stratosphériques* (Stratospheric Shots); 13. *Les Métèques au poteau* (Aliens to the Gallows!); 14. *Les Tricolores sur Munich* (The Tricolor over Munich); 15. *Le Rayon orange.*

V. *Combats navals* (Naval Battles), comprising: 16. *La Bataille de Franche-Comté* (The Battle of Franche-Comté); 17. *La Fin d'un reître* (The End of a Thug); 18. *Combats dans la Mer du Nord* (Battles in the North Sea); 19. *Vers la Ruhr* (Toward the Ruhr); 20. *La Bataille de Belgique* (The Battle of Belgium).

VI. *L'Épopée* (The Epic), comprising: 21. *Le Victoire des ailes* (Winged Victory); 22. *Vers le grand duel* (Toward the Great Duel); 23. *La Ruée sur le Rhin* (The Rush over the Rhine); 24. *L'Aube du grand choc* (The Dawn of the Great Shock); 25. *L'Épopée.*

L'Héroïque aventure advertised itself as "the most moving, the most dramatic anticipation that has been written since the remarkable work of Captain Danrit (Commander Driant). . . . It's an unforgettable epic!"[95] Émile Driant (1855–1916), author of a monumental series of future-war novels, was a Saint-Cyr graduate, son-in-law of General Boulanger, and hero of the Battle of Verdun. He had been a friend of Maurice Barrès but not necessarily of Pouvourville, who in *La Voie rationnelle* had scorned Driant's assertions about Chinese secret societies and Martinism.[96] With the advantage of hindsight (Danrit having cast England as France's coming enemy) Pouvourville updated the genre to send out a wake-up call to more and younger readers than he had ever addressed.

Another motive for the project may lie in the theory and practice of magic, defined by Matgioi's contemporary Aleister Crowley (1875–1947) as "the science and art of causing change to occur in conformity with the will," and using as its chief instrument the imagination.* During the hours of concentration with which every writer is to some extent familiar, Pouvourville might have been working on what magic calls the inner planes, imagining the coming war in minute detail and bringing it to the desired conclusion. Whether or not one believes that magic "works" is irrelevant. I am merely suggesting that a man who was no stranger to occultism may have had some such intention.

While he was preparing his adventure series, Pouvourville found the time—and, more surprisingly, the urge—to write a short book about a favorite Catholic saint: Thérèse of Lisieux (1873–1897), known as the "Little Flower."[97]

Cover of Pouvourville's
Sainte Thérèse de Lisieux (1934)

---

*Crowley preferred the spelling "magick."

This anomalous production seems like the eruption of a "shadow" in the Jungian sense: the suppressed counterpart of the impassive warrior, the metaphysical geometer, and disparager of sentimental religion. "If Albert de Pouvourville is still alive, Matgioi is surely dead!" wrote Guénon to his friend Gary de Lacroze.[98] The book bears the *Nihil obstat* and *Imprimatur* of the Roman Church's censors and prefaces by two high ecclesiastics. It exudes Catholic piety, relating the saint's life and the miraculous cures worked by her intercession (with dates and medical details), and praising her zeal for missionary work in infidel lands like China. Intensely chauvinistic, it boasts of France being the "Eldest Daughter of the Church" and even the "favorite people of the Eternal." Thérèse joins Saints Geneviève, Clothilde, and Joan of Arc as the national protectors on whom France can rely in times of peril. The only explanation I can offer is that Pouvourville, like the Daoist *phap* adjusting to his student's level, was assuming the appropriate mask and voice to prepare a different group for the coming war: committed Catholics for whom Thérèse's example of selfless love and the acceptance of suffering would be their best hope.

Matgioi is a fascinating character, as this introduction has shown, and a man of his time, place, and circumstances—as are we. There are truths, however, that transcend his conditions, and ours. They are the natural gems whose value far exceeds their manmade settings. But they have to be dug for, and not all, however earnest, have the patience to search them out. Some readers may find the preoccupation with the *Yijing* irrelevant, the explanations confusing. That should not deter them from this unfamiliar and rich territory, to which the following outlines may serve as signposts.

In Chapter 1, "The Primordial Tradition," the author declares that he is opening up the treasure of this Tradition for the modern West. While the Tradition itself is as old as humanity, its earliest formulation is ascribed to the mythical Chinese emperor Fuxi, in the fourth pre-Christian millennium. The Far Eastern peoples have never lost their connection with it, with fortunate consequences for social and personal life. The first chapter contrasts this Tradition ("Religion") with later degradations of it ("religions"), with their obligations, sanctions, exclusivism, state control, and paid clergy. The people's moral conduct is better served by the natural philosophy of Confucius. The Far Eastern peoples believe absolutely in the Supreme Being, the divine order (Heaven), and man's place in it, but do not seek any personal relationship: Tradition suffices.

Chapter 2, "The First Monument of Knowledge," relates how, for the Far Easterners, the most ancient books by definition contain the best of teachings. Of Fuxi's three books, two are lost; the *Yijing* remains. Humanity originated at the Navel of the Earth in the mountains of central Asia, where it had a single language and a single script. In time, climate change or curiosity drove men down to the plains. There they divided into four races distinguished by skin color. Much later, Fuxi adapted the Tradition to human comprehension. Since the original script was lost, he used geometric symbols, representing the double principle of reality, active and passive, by a straight line and a broken line. Their combinations form the sixty-four hexagrams of the *Yijing*. The nonverbal, symbolic nature of Chinese ideograms yielded multiple interpretations and applications of the hexagrams and their early commentaries. This is disquieting to those accustomed to the precise and narrow statements of Greek philosophy. Only long absorption in the sources can yield the proper intuitions.

Chapter 3, "The Graphics of God," presupposes an impersonal God that is beyond being, yet the cause of all existence. If the latter is represented by the numbers from 1 to infinity, then God is the incomprehensible but necessary zero. In Fuxi's symbolism, God's "active Perfection" is represented by the indefinite straight line, while the broken line represents the "passive Perfection" of multiplicity and the manifested universe. Their combination yields the eight trigrams of Fuxi, which together with their reflections make the sixty-four hexagrams of the *Yijing*. Studying them brings Westerners back to the sacred science that we once shared with China and India, before it was disfigured by notions of an anthropomorphic God.

Chapter 4, "The Symbols of the Word," allegorizes the six lines of the hexagram through the Myth of the Dragon. The Dragon is identical to the Logos of Greek philosophy, the Word of Christian theology, the activity of Heaven in Daoism. It ascends in six stages: (1) nonaction, (2) possibility of manifestation, (3) manifestation in multiplicity of forms, (4) indeterminacy or freedom, (5) completeness of creation, and (6) current cycle of humanity with its nostalgia for primordial perfection. This is reflected on the human level as a set of ethical and practical guidelines, first for the gifted or superior man, then for the simple citizen.

Chapter 5, "The Forms of the Universe," presents a four-part scheme, symbolized by the "tetragram of Wen Wang" (actually, the first four characters of the latter's commentary on the hexagrams). This contains the whole of Daoist cosmology, consisting of: (1) Initial Cause of all beings, (2) Liberty or Activity in their modification or growth, (3) the Good as goal of their action, and (4) Perfection as their ultimate development. There is no place here for a principle of evil. From the human point of view, the process can be seen as entry into the "current of forms" and exit from it. This applies both to humanity as a whole and to the individual, who is of less concern to the Far Eastern mentality.

Chapter 6, "The Laws of Evolution," focuses on the human state, one of the universe's innumerable forms, and on earthly humanity as one modification of that form. It issues from Perfection, passes through all modes of being following the Law of Harmony, and is reintegrated in Perfection. There are no falls on the way, though we are subject to limitations, including in our understanding of these matters. We may evolve alongside others in a "fraternity of spirits," but do not reincarnate in earthly humanity: there is no repetition of forms. This chapter introduces the important symbolism of the helix or spiral, inscribed on a cylinder or a cone. It represents the course of the universe from its origin in the Principle of Activity, its progress through the Principle of the Good, to its reintegration in the Perfection from which it came. This is likewise the destiny of all beings.

Chapter 7, "The Destinies of Humanity," symbolizes humanity as a single turn of the helix, which ends at a higher level from where it began. There is nothing special about the human form; it is just one of a multitude of episodes in which we participate and will give place to others. Neither is it confined to this planet, whose current humanity is but one point on the turn. Chance does not exist: its course is governed by the laws of Harmony and the Good, the latter determining its upward direction. The human form is utterly distinct from animal forms and did not evolve from them: it has always been present. Eternal damnation is a fiction with no place in original traditions. Consideration of the final transformation leads to imagining the cylinder as a cone, with its vertex as the locus of the Will of Heaven. Once that is reached, we might imagine an inverted cone expanding from its vertex. Does that mean that after Nirvana is attained, another cycle begins? Possibly. At all events, all paths lead to the happy and total end of Reintegration.

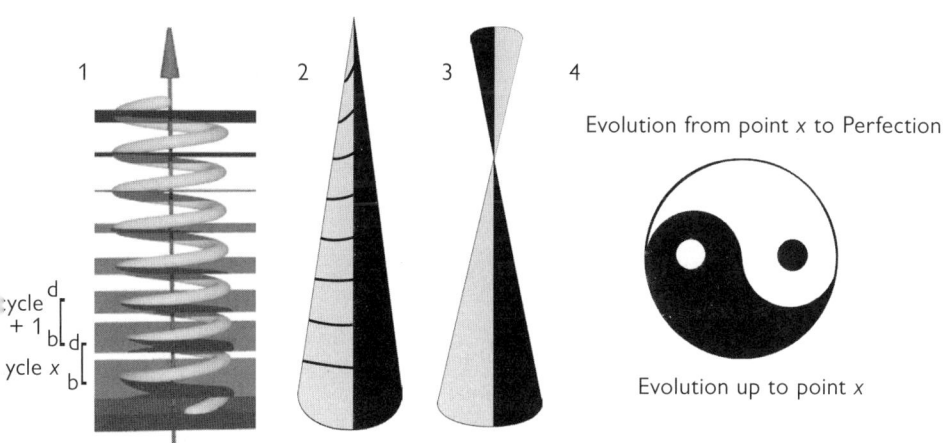

Evolution from point *x* to Perfection

Evolution up to point *x*

1: Evolution as a cylinder; 2: Evolutions as a cone, culminating in perfection; 3: Possible emergence of another universe; 4: Yin-yang as the view of evolution from the point of view of perfection.

Chapter 8, "The Conditions of the Individual," is the longest and the most relevant to our concerns. It takes the symbol of the Yin-Yang to represent the individual's destiny, the two semicircles representing his emission from, and reintegration in, Perfection. This manifests the principles of Causality, Activity, and Harmony, but not that of the Good. In universal evolution there is no freedom; humans are not free to choose either their birth or death. But in between, the attraction of the Will of Heaven is not felt. Consequently, humans do have freedom and can act for better or worse. This alone is where good and evil are created, along with their repercussions in this or another life. But since evil does not exist as an independent entity, no punishment can be eternal.

Birth and death are identical in nature, each being the exit from one state and the entrance into another state. We feel that birth is preferable or superior to death. But due to the attraction of the Will of Heaven (symbolized by the upward-tending spiral), the passage of death will occur at a higher level than the passage of birth. This is proven by study of the human aggregate of body, soul, and spirit. By joining those in an individual, birth provided something superior to the previous state, namely spirit. Death removes the material body, the lowest element of the aggregate, and provides some higher spiritual element.

What joins those elements to make an individual is the Personality, a completely distinct entity. It is immortal, containing an indefinite number of individuals whose birth and death do not affect it. The Law of Rebirths refers not to individuals but to the Personality, which goes from one existence to another until its reintegration. This is where we should place our aspirations.

Even though death is a beneficent passage to a higher state, we resist it, and weep for the departed. We are not mourning the body, which has gone back to enter other forms. It is because of the human emotions that have been gathered in a lifetime and which now vanish. These constitute the soul, which dissolves into the psychic world, never to be reconstituted. We feel the emotion not in our body or reason, but precisely in our soul, and most strongly toward those whose emotions have penetrated our own.

The eternal personality absorbs all its individualities, the heritage of former cycles. Nothing of them is absolutely lost. A human life profits us, both for our evolution and for the formation of the personality. All positive emotions contribute to the goal of evolution, which is unity. Thus, personalities that were emotionally close will remain so in future cycles. Our present affinities are the result of past cycles and promise ever-closer union.

Lastly, Matgioi offers a practical corollary to these metaphysical studies. Our current state as humans affords the opportunity to conform to the Will of Heaven. This can be done by (1) relying on its principle, (2) disengagement from all passions, (3) logically and rationally deducing its consequences, and (4) following Heaven's rule of perfectible reason. Given a pure heart, any errors we commit are only due to the imperfection of the human state. Every step we take—every effort, thought, and even dream—is part of our inevitable spiral ascent to the Center and the Truth.

Chapter 9, "The Instruments of Divination," is an instruction manual for the use and interpretation of the *Yijing*, which Matgioi admits is unusable without the oral teaching. Thanks to the quality of later scholarship and the quantity of popular literature on the *Yijing*, its interest is solely historical. Matgioi takes the opportunity for a tribute to its translator Paul-Louis-Félix Philastre, often mentioned in the present book. This diplomat and scholar served, like Pouvourville, in Indochina, and in 1874 negotiated the Treaty of Saigon between the French protectorate and the local rulers. Matgioi was a warm defender of Philastre against accusations of having overreached his authority, which put an end to his diplomatic career.

An analysis of the influence of Matgioi's *Voie métaphysique* on René Guénon is beyond the scope of this Introduction. In any case, the work stands or falls on its own merits. These reside mainly in Chapters 6, 7, and 8, by which point Matgioi has cut loose from his Daoist pretext to present his own vision of reality. Like earlier metaphysicians—Plato's "divided line" and Robert Fludd's intersecting pyramids come to mind—he uses a geometrical figure as a visual aid. Whereas Guénon emphasized the devolutionary cycle of four Ages or Yugas, Matgioi takes the broader, evolutionary view, symbolized by the rising volutes of the spiral. Each turn would then comprise an entire cycle, its components apparently declining but each cycle starting "higher" than the previous one. This would be the macrocosmic equivalent of the individual's life, which is in a sense a decline from the Golden Age of infancy to debility and death, but for whom death to this state is birth into a higher one.

A NOTE ON THE TRANSLATION

Because *La Voie métaphysique* is in part a historic document, representing French scholarship and orthography of the late nineteenth century, I have generally retained Matgioi's italics, capitalization, and spelling of Chinese and Vietnamese names and terms. I have however replaced his frequent references to "Yellows" by "Far Easterners," except in Chapter Two, which adopts Fabre d'Olivet's scheme of four primordial races identified by color.[99]

I owe a longstanding debt of thanks to Dr. Jean-Pierre Laurant, whose seminars at the École Pratique des Hautes Études in 1985–86 encouraged my early explorations of the French esoteric traditions; and a more recent one to Dr. David Marino, for his scholarship and insights on Matgioi. Any shortcomings in the present work are entirely my own. I am also grateful to Ehud Sperling and Jon Graham of Inner Traditions for supporting this and many other projects over the years.

Joscelyn Godwin
Hamilton, N.Y.

Joscelyn Godwin was born in England and educated at Cambridge and Cornell Universities (PhD in Musicology, 1969). His writings, editions, and translations concern the spiritual and cosmological aspects of music (*Harmonies of Heaven and Earth, Cosmic Music, The Mystery of the Seven Vowels*, and editions of Hans Kayser and Michael Maier) and the Western esoteric tradition (*The Pagan Dream of the Renaissance, The Theosophical Enlightenment, Arktos, Atlantis and the Cycles of Time, Symbols in the Wilderness, Universal Magic in the Age of Enlightenment*, and books on Robert Fludd and Athanasius Kircher). The present work complements his translation of René Guénon's *The Multiple States of Being*, and his *Music and the Occult: French Musical Philosophies, 1750–1950*.

NOTES

1. Jean-Pierre Laurant, *Matgioi, un aventurier Taoïste* (Dervy-Livres, 1982), 17–18. The following biographical information is mostly drawn from this source. Dr. Laurant informs me that Guy de Pouvourville also had a Vietnamese connection: he was one of the last pilots to land at (and succeed in leaving) Dien Bien Phu in 1954. The French national archives document Albert de Pouvourville's birth certificate and his Legion of Honor titles.

2. *Bulletin du Musée historique de Mulhouse* 9 (1884): 97. The other son was Adolphe René, who died in 1892, aged 24 (Laurant, *Matgioi*, 28).

3. Albert de Pouvourville, *Les Terres meurtries* (Berger-Levrault, 1915), 57–59.

4. Pouvourville, *Les Terres meurtries*, 86.

5. Stanislas de Guaita, *Au seuil du mystère* (Durville, 1915), 5.

6. Pouvourville, *Chasseurs de pirates! . . . (Les Livres de la Brousse)* (Éditions du Monde Nouveau, 1928), 107, 191.

7. Mat Gioi, *Le Tonkin actuel, 1887–1890* (Savine, 1892), 281.

8. Pouvourville, *Chasseurs*, 151. Like some other claims, this one is not supported by the evidence, especially as collected in Davide Marino's studies: "Albert de Pouvourville's *Occultisme Colonial*," *Numen* 71 (2024): 71–93; "The Daoist Who Wasn't: Albert de Pouvourville, Matgioi, Nguyen Van Cang and the Problem of Indochinese Masters in *fin de siècle* Occultism," in *Appropriating the Dao: The Euro-American Esoteric Reception of China*, ed. Lukas K. Pokorny (Bloomsbury, 2024), 83–108; "The Path to Gnosis: A Microhistory," *Vienna Journal of East Asian Studies* 16.1 (2024): 1–28.

9. Thus described in the "definitive edition," Albert de Pouvourville (Matgioi), *L'Annam sanglant* (Michaud, 1912), 9.

10. Laurant, *Matgioi*, 31.

11. Symbolism as explained in Théophane [Léon Champrenaud], *Matgioi et son rôle dans les sociétés secrètes chinoises: Étude suivie d'un résumé de la métaphysique Taoïste* (Librairie Hermétique, 1910), 5.

12. Pouvourville, *Chasseurs*, 41.

13. Albert de Pouvourville (Matgioi), *Le Cinquième bonheur* (Michaud, 1911), 312.

14. Explained in Pouvourville, *Chasseurs*, 195.

15. Pouvourville, *Chasseurs*, 257.

16. Matgioi, *Deux années de luttes, 1890–1891* (Savine, 1892), 31–32.

17. Matgioi, *Deux années*, dedication page.

18. Laurant, *Matgioi*, 31.

19. Albert de Pouvourville (Matgioi), *L'Art indochinois* (Quantin, 1894, and reeditions).

20. E.g., Ananda K. Coomaraswamy, *Christian and Oriental Philosophy of Art* (Dover, 1956); Titus Burckhardt, *Sacred Art in East and West: Its Principles and Methods,* trans. Lord Northbourne (Perennial, 1967).

21. Pouvourville, *L'Art indochinois*, 265.

22. Pouvourville, *L'Art indochinois*, 133.

23. Matgioi, *Le Taoïsme et les sociétés secrètes chinoises* (Chamuel, 1897), 7.

24. Matgioi, *Le Taoïsme*, 6.

25. Matgioi, *Le Taoïsme*, 19.

26. Massimo Introvigne, "In Search of China's Secret Societies. 1. Matgioi and the Esoteric Connection," *Bitter Winter: A Magazine on Religious Liberty and Human Rights*, 2 June 2022. Accessed online.

27. Matgioi, *Le Taoïsme*, 7–14.

28. Albert de Pouvourville (Matgioi), *Le Maître des sentences: Roman asiatique* (Ollendorf, 1899), 211.

29. Matgioi, *Le Maître*, 190.

30. Laurant, *Matgioi*, 41, n. 9.

31. Théophane, *Matgioi et son rôle dans les sociétés secrètes chinoises: Étude suivie d'un résumé de la métaphysique Taoïste* (Paris: Librarie Hermétique, 1910), 26.

32. Laurant, *Matgioi*, 41.

33. On Bailly's bookshop and esoteric connections, see Joscelyn Godwin, *Music and the Occult: French Musical Philosophies 1750–1950* (University of Rochester Press, 1995), 151–75; also Edward Lockspeiser, *Debussy, His Life and Mind* (Cassell, 1965), II:273–76.

34. *La Haute Science* II (1894): 7–32.

35. *La Haute Science* II (1894): 239–70, 361–72, 385–95.

36. *La Haute Science* II (1894): 258.

37. *La Haute Science* II (1894): 385.

38. *Le Tao de Laotseu traduit du chinois par Matgioi (Albert de Pouvourville)* (Librairie de l'Art Indépendant, 1894), 25.

39. *The Sacred Books of China: The Texts of Tâoism, Part 1: The Tâo Teh King*, trans. James Legge (Clarendon, 1891), 61.

40. Matgioi, *La Voie Rationnelle* (Société d'Éditions Contemporaines / Bodin, 1907), 45.

41. Laurant, *Matgioi*, 70 and n. 5. On p. 72 he compares it with the respected French translation of J. J. L. Duyvendak.

42. MoGd, "Les sept éléments de l'homme et la pathogénie chinoise (avec figures)," *L'Initiation* 23.9 (June 1894): 236–49; 24.10 (July 1894): 51–60; 24.11 (Aug. 1894): 150–68; 26.4 (Jan. 1895): 29–45.

43. Matgioi, *Les Sept éléments de l'homme et la pathogénie chinoise* (Chamuel, 1895); *L'Opium, sa pratique* (Chamuel, 1895); *Le Traité des influences errantes de Quangdzu* (Bibliothèque de la Haute-Science, 1896); *Le Taoïsme et les sociétés secrètes* (Chamuel, 1897).

44. Lacking access to the original, this is based on the excerpt in Jacques Borgé and Nicolas Viasnoff, eds., *Archives de l'Indochine* (Trinckvel, 1995), 34–37, there attributed to "De Pourville."

45. Matgioi, *Le Traité des influences errantes*, 5.

46. Marriage date from *Annuaire de la noblesse de France* 52 (1896), 557.

47. Laurant, *Matgioi*, 33.

48. Laurant, *Matgioi*, 43, n. 15.

49. Laurant, *Matgioi*, 23–24.

50. For an analysis of the two periodicals *La Voie* and *La Gnose*, and the background to them, see Marino, "The Path to Gnosis."

51. Marino, "The Daoist Who Wasn't," 85–95.

52. Pouvourville, *L'Annamite* (Larose, 1932), 68–82

53. Pouvourville, *L'Annamite*, 81.

54. Allusion to Montesquieu's *Lettres persanes* (1721).

55. Paul Chacornac, *La Vie simple de René Guénon* (Les Éditions Traditionnelles, 1958), 41–43. See Marino, "The Daoist Who Wasn't," 93–95.

56. The first, 1907 edition of *La Voie rationnelle* contains two items omitted from Chacornac's oft-reprinted 1941 edition: the preface by Abbé Alta and, as sole appendix, *Les Influences errantes*.

57. Laurant, *Matgioi*, 57, n. 13.

58. From "Declaration des Statuts de l'Église Gnostique," in Simon-Théophane, *Les Enseignements secrets de la Gnose* (Société d'Édition Contemporaine et Librairie Bodin, 1907; facsimile edition: Archè, 1999), 74. For later claimants to the lineage, see the history section of the L'Église Gnostique Apostolique website.

59. Information from Robin Waterfield, *René Guénon and the Future of the West* (Crucible, 1987), 35.

60. Simon-Théophane, *Enseignements secrets*, 1.

61. Simon-Théophane, *Enseignements secrets*, 7.

62. Francis Warrain, *Le Synthèse concrète: Étude métaphysique de la vie* (Librairie Générale des Sciences Occultes / Bibliothèque Chacornac, 1910).

63. See Marcel Clavelle, *Alcuni ricordi su René Guénon e la rivista "Études traditionnelles." Dossier confidenziale inedito* (L'Arcano, 2007), 58–59.

64. See, however, my Introduction to Petrus Talemarianus, *Natural Architecture*, trans. Ariel Godwin (Sacred Science Institute, 2007), vii–xii. On this group, see also Godwin, *Music and the Occult*, 117–22.

65. See Marino, "The Path to Gnosis."

66. Albert de Pouvourville, *L'Opium et l'alcool en Indochine* (Établissements Généraux d'Imprimérie, 1910).

67. The following account is based on Jean Robin, *René Guénon, témoin de la tradition* (Trédaniel, 1986), 52–53.

68. Jean-Pierre Laurant, *Le Sens caché dans l'oeuvre de René Guénon* (L'Âge d'Homme, 1976), 44–48.

69. Laurant, *Matgioi*, 62.

70. T Palingénius, "Le Démiurge," *La Gnose*, 1.1 (Nov. 1909): 7–10; 1.2 (Dec. 1909): 25–27; 1.3 (Jan. 1910): 46-49; 1.4 (Feb. 1910): 67–68. Reprinted in René Guénon, *Mélanges* (Gallimard, 1976), 10–25. The "T" stands for the Greek letter *tau*, denoting a Gnostic bishop. On Guénon's changing attitude to Gnosticism, see Jean Borella, "Gnose et gnosticisme chez René Guénon," in *René Guénon*, ed. Pierre-Marie Sigaud (L'Âge d'Homme, 1984), 92–122.

71. These include the Demiurge itself (*Enseignements secrets* [hereafter *ESG*], 16, 42), Being and Nonbeing (*ESG, 15*), Good and Evil (*ESG, 43*), Adam Kadmon (*ESG, 24, 31*), the individual (*ESG, 38*), and liberation (*ESG, 56*).

72. Matgioi, "L'erreur métaphysique des religions à forme sentimentale," *La Gnose* 2.3 (March 1911): 77–80.

73. Robin, *René Guénon*, 70. On Guénon's activities during this period, and his relations to Matgioi, see Louis le Maistre, *L'Énigme René Guénon et les "Supérieurs Inconnus": Contribution à l'étude de l'histoire du mondiale "souterraine"* (Archè, 2004), 748–56.

74. Four complete editions are: Saint-Yves d'Alveydre, "L'Archéomètre," *La Gnose*, various issues 1.9 (July–Aug. 1910) to 3.2 (Feb. 1912); *L'Archéomètre: Clef de toutes les religions et de toutes les sciences de l'antiquité; Réforme synthétique de tous les arts contemporains* (Dorbon-Aîné, 1911 or 1912; facsimile: Gutenberg Reprints, 1979); *The Archeometer*, English translation by Ariel Godwin (Sacred Science Institute, 2008); and the Bulgarian translation by Maria Doncheva (Mont, 2016). On Guénon's notes and his relation to Saint-Yves' work, see Nicolas Séd, "Les Notes de Palingénius pour "l'Archéomètre," in Jean-Pierre Laurant and Paul Barbanegra, eds., *René Guénon* (Éditions de l'Herne, 1985), 117–35.

75. See my Introduction to Saint-Yves d'Alveydre, *The Kingdom of Agarttha: A Journey into the Hollow Earth*, trans. Jon E. Graham (Inner Traditions, 2008), 1–27.

76. On Aguéli's Sufism (and also for insights on Matgioi) see Mark Sedgwick, *Against the Modern World: Traditionalism and the Secret Intellectual History of the Twentieth Century* (Oxford University Press, 2004), 59–63, and his *Anarchist, Artist, Sufi: The Politics, Painting, and Esotericism of Ivan Aguéli* (Bloomsbury Academic, 2021).

77. Simon-Théophane, *Les Enseignements secrets*, 37.

78. According to Sedgwick, *Against the Modern World*, 60.

79. Sedgwick, *Against the Modern World*, 62. Thanks to Davide Marino for making this point about Daoism.

80. Pouvourville, *Chasseurs*, 185.

81. Bibliography in Laurant, *Matgioi*, 104–106.

82. Laurant, *Matgioi*, 20.

83. Laurant, *Matgioi*, 19.

84. Laurant, *Matgioi*, 19.

85. Laurant, *Matgioi*, 53, n. 1.

86. Laurant, *Matgioi*, 21.

87. Laurant, *Matgioi*, 21.

88. Laurant, *Le Sens caché*, 67.

89. René Guénon, *Le Théosophisme, histoire d'une pseudo-religion* (Nouvelle Librairie Nationale, 1921); *L'Erreur spirite* (Rivière, 1923).

90. René Guénon, *Introduction générale à l'étude des doctrines hindoues* (Rivière, 1921).

91. Matgioi, Preface to H. P. Blavatsky, *Au pays des montagnes bleues*, trans. Mark Semenoff (Éditions du Monde Moderne, 1926).

92. Matgioi, *Le Taoïsme*, 4. The maxim also appears in Chapter 1 of the present volume on p. 63.

93. On this relationship and the possible causes of Guénon's exile, see Le Maistre, *L'Énigme René Guénon*, 780–86.

94. Quoted from verso of covers of the series.

95. Back cover of Albert de Pouvourville, *L'Héroïque aventure*, I: *Les Navigyres* (Baudinière, 1934).

96. Matgioi, *La Voie rationnelle*, 337–38.

97. Albert de Pouvourville, *Sainte Thérèse de Lisieux, protectrice des peuples* (Éditions du Lys, 1934).

98. Laurant, *Matgioi*, 93.

99. See Fabre d'Olivet, *De l'État social de l'homme* (Brière, 1822); English edition: *Hermeneutic Interpretation of the Origin of the Social State of Man*, trans. Nayán Louise Redfield (Putnam's Sons, 1915), especially bk. I, ch. 1.

THE METAPHYSICAL WAY

MATGIOI

(1905)

Explanatory Note
(From the 1905 Edition)

This is not the kind of preface in which I pompously present the Oriental Tradition for Western criticism. Where spiritual matters are concerned, it would be more courteous, logical, and normal to present the West to the East—so long as the latter consented.

Nor do I want to oppose two doctrines to one another, or rather two human teachings based on one doctrine. I simply thought that in an era of efforts to trace the sources of human knowledge in search of the almost unpolluted truth, it would be good to represent the primordial and traditional source of all knowledge, the initial river to which all humanity is tributary. I have drawn it out of the limbo from which it is a delicate matter to disengage it: first, because the obligatory Far Eastern sojourn is more often made today for cutting off heads than for deciphering and understanding texts; then, because the ideography in which the Tradition is contained is practically unknown to the White race; and, lastly, because by my count there are exactly five Europeans, one recently dead, who have received, along with the material means of reading it, the intellectual means of comprehending the depth of their reading.

I have decided to divide this work into three parts. The present one, *The Metaphysical Way*, explains the Tradition's principles and its philosophical and cosmogonic movement. The second, *The Rational Way*, will explain the Tradition's systematization with Taoism, or Laotseu's "Way and Virtue of Reason." The third, *The Social Way*, will show the Tradition's adaptation with the political and communist philosophy of Kongtzeu (called Confucius by the Christian missionaries).*

This is a very sensitive task, which I can claim to have acquitted, if not successfully, at least with great care. Its fruits will probably not be very agreeable to European taste. However, I must admit that for practical if not admirable purposes, I have often used Western phraseology to facilitate understanding of the sacred and ancient Far Eastern texts, and rather than using the reasoning appropriate to them, I have used methods suited to the readers' minds, whenever the two lead to an identical conclusion.

I have felt justified in this because the teachings of the Metaphysical Way would have been incomprehensible without commentaries. Thus, I have adapted my commentaries directly to the Western mentality, rather than forcing theories in an Eastern language to be translated into a Western language, which is always laborious, though it would have been easier for me to expound.

I will not do this in *The Rational Way* or in *The Social Way*, because there are no arguments to be added to the teachings of Laotseu and Kongtzeu, only some clarifications. Beside my own preference, I have been led to this strict transposition by seeing the comical results of some recent pseudo-translators, who have thought fit to embellish and improve the *Book of the Way* [*Daodejing*], and in so doing have not even the excuse of being members of the Institut de France.

If, after the arduous reading or outright rejection of these difficult but marvelous doctrines, I am denied the merit of being elegant,

---

*[French Publisher's note to the Third Edition (1956): The third volume announced by the author, *La Voie sociale*, has never been published, and we do not know whether it was ever written.]

interesting, and agreeable, at least I can testify that I have always been a respectful interpreter of the tradition, and a scrupulous and pious son of the masters who taught it to me.

This testimony sets my conscience at rest, which has always been, and remains, my sole concern. For the success of this enterprise, which is merely the local exposition of a doctrine, matters nothing to a Word that knows itself to be eternal.

MATGIOI

1
The Primordial Tradition

The present-day religions of the Far Eastern peoples* comprise a host of different elements. One may see only a popular blend that emerged from three parent sources: primitive religion, Taoism, and Confucianism. These three influences, amalgamated over centuries to better or worse effect, constitute the traditional religion of the empire, while their three corresponding liturgies form the body of official and popular ceremonies.

Travelers, missionaries, and all the strangers to the Far Eastern races who have judged the traditional Chinese situation from this external viewpoint, have taken its appearance for reality. Besides, even if they had tried to penetrate further (for which they had neither time nor inclination), they would have been halted by the guardians of the Primordial Tradition, which is not even popularized among the Chinese people, and all the more hidden from the far-off barbarians.

It is easy to misunderstand those who wish to remain unknown. That is what Western scholars have done vis-à-vis the Far Eastern savants, and with greater impunity since none was there to respond to them. Believing that they could be dispensed with, they were ignored. Consequently, the most venerable Western tradition tried to reach the beginning of time by climbing Jacob's Ladder, and for want of anything

---

*[Matgioi habitually refers to the peoples of the Far East as *Jaunes*, "Yellows," by analogy to "Blacks" and "Whites" as referring to broad racial groups. —*Trans.*]

better, fastened onto that Judaism which is merely a bloodthirsty parody of the ancient Hindu cults, and onto that Mosaism which is only an Egyptian adaptation washed out in the Red Sea.

Nowadays we know of better and nobler origins. If Europe's colonial conquests had had no other result, they would no less deserve the gratitude of the human spirit. For they have unveiled to it, albeit unconsciously, the traditions carefully concealed behind the Great Walls by civilizations most closed and contrary to our mentalities.

I shall attempt to open up this treasure for the twentieth Western century: a treasure hidden for five thousand years and unknown even to some of its guardians. To begin with, I shall set out its main characters, thanks to which it appears as the First Tradition and, consequently, the authentic one. I will then show, through the human and tangible proof left us by its authors, how the monuments of this tradition go back to an epoch when forests covered Europe and even Western Asia, where humans were hardly distinguishable from the bears and wolves, as hairy as them and eating raw flesh.

Three thousand seven hundred years before Christ (i.e., 2300 before Moses), the enigmatic emperor Fohi wrote the metaphysical and cosmogonic arcana that served as basis for the *Yiking*.* He declared with great respect that he drew his teaching from the past, calling it very learned, very prudent, and very difficult to determine.

Moreover, he realized that one day, for future races, his own epoch would be a past one, just as abstruse and difficult to define.

Fohi dated his work not by a conventional epoch, or the name of a ruler whose fame and even memory would be erased by time, but by a *solar and stellar situation*, which he describes in every detail, and which future astronomers could date beyond all possible error. Thus, whereas the Hebrew patriarchs gave the Benedictines much useless labor, for all their great books and intense studies, the exact date of Fohi and his

---

*It is important to state, once and for all, that "Fohi" is neither a man nor a myth, but the term for an intellectual aggregate (as, incidentally, was "Hermes").

Yiking could easily be found by handing a telescope to one of Camille Flammarion's* numerous disciples. Doubtless, Fohi feared neither the verification nor the dissent of posterity. We emphasize this marvelous precaution, not only to show how perfect the science of Astronomy had become in those times, but to demonstrate at a stroke the practical, ingenious, logical, and unclouded mind of the Chinese magi 5,000 years ago: a mind that distinguishes them from all the reformers of peoples who came later on the earth, yet lived only legends and wrote only parables.

For the half-billion individuals who populate the Far East, whatever the outward form of their beliefs, when it concerns the origin of things, the divine essence, and the relations of heaven to earth and to men there has never been any divine revelation nor intervention from on high—not at any epoch, historical or legendary (and Chinese history is authentic for 5,000 years). There is nothing "supernatural" in the books, the commentaries, or the traditions. The idea does not occur, the word is not spoken. No patriarch has seen the Lord, like Moses; no man has conversed with angels, like Mohammed; no saint has achieved eternal perfection in this life, like the Buddha; no God has descended to earth, like the Messiah.

To reason with the severe logic of the Chinese tradition, to comprehend its undeniable clarity, one must insist strongly on this original distinction. It declares itself human and claims none but human knowledge, to the exclusion of all divine mystery and even of every metaphysical postulate.

Despite a widespread linguistic error, a "revelation" is the exact contrary of an "explanation." To reveal is the opposite of unveil, just as re-cover is the opposite of dis-cover. A revelation is a cloud placed over the truth, a cloud whose forms suit the moral aesthetic of the moment. Not to mince words, it is a lie, fit for the sentiments and needs of the hour in which it is formulated, and destined in future to be argued

---

*[Camille Flammarion (1842–1925), eminent French astronomer and psychical researcher. —*Trans.*]

over, denied, and replaced, just as the sentiments that gave it birth are transformed.

Is there, then, any need for God? And on the contrary, shouldn't one say that the supposition of "revelations" made by a god who speaks or walks and lives is a consequence of unconscious anthropomorphism, which was and remains the sovereign master of the theogonic concepts of a good part of the human race?

But the masters of Far Eastern thought had no need for heaven's help in dissipating errors or creating symbols.

Their peoples, satisfied by the truth that they had never lost, needed no fancy covering for it. They did not demand the manifestation of God, because they were still too close to it to have already forgotten or mistaken it.* In the intact Tradition and the words of those who transmitted it, they saw clearly heaven itself and its work. Satisfied by being able to comprehend the Father from whom they descended, they felt no urgency for a divinity to appear before their eyes in more or less tangible form to impose a doctrine on them, manmade yet full of mysteries defying common sense and overturning human logic.

Thus, the primordial tradition was able to perpetuate itself among the Far Eastern peoples, to whom we owe the first monuments of writing and science, without any need to triumph through the violence of a god or a heavenly intervention. For that very reason we should recognize it as being appropriate *in itself* for the human race, and thus intact and true.

This tradition, which is neither unveiled nor revealed by a god, which is not dogmatized or decreed by the official or officious representatives of a divinity, has none of the characteristics of things that are *a priori* and above human nature and, consequently, beyond human discussion.

Let us now outline the practical consequences of this undisputed origin of the Primordial Tradition for the daily life of the Far Eastern peoples. Beside satisfying logic and facilitating rational study,

---

*[The neuter pronoun (lacking in French) answers to Matgioi's impersonal concept of God. — *Trans.*]

it enabled the Chinese to enjoy an uncommon degree of wellbeing, due to the modesty of their first sages, who were also their first emperors. These felt no need to win honor and obedience by making their decrees emerge from a Sibyl's cave or fall from a cloud-covered mountain. Theirs were a happy people, not forced into a perpetual struggle between their reason and their heart, always having at hand the help and the voice of Heaven. In their sacred tradition they found the means for present prosperity and future felicity. No mysterious power instilled the fear of a terrible and revengeful sovereign on high, nor did the thought of death, natural and inevitable, poison their earthly life with the anguish of the unknown.

Every Far Easterner is as attached to this Tradition as to his family, his land, and his own blood, even if he does not fully comprehend it, for it sums up the whole intellectual and moral heritage of the Ancestors. This Tradition does not claim a divine source (at least not direct and particular to the race); it imposes no theocratic doctrine, lays down no religious dogmas. As a direct consequence, all the *religions*, all the liturgies that more or less flourish in the Far East have no traditional origin. They do not participate in the absolute and infrangible character of a transmitted heritage. They are nothing more than *options*, unable to claim the obedience owed to things handed down as certainties, nor the respect owed to those handed down as ancient. The Tradition in person imposes itself solely through its clarity and the all-powerful virtue of its past. How could religions, being more or less pure translations of this tradition for easy adaptation to the populace, dare to usurp this character of obligatory certitude, which the Tradition itself nowhere imposes?

"Love Religion—mistrust religions." This maxim, inscribed on the temple fronts and in the minds of men, is the only advice given to the races in question—and this advice is not a command. But it defines with a brevity of unequaled clarity how "Religion" is precisely the Primordial Tradition, exclusively human, and how "religions" with celestial interventions are an easier but less exact means to ascend to Religion.

One can see immediately the deep consequences of so logical, simple, and natural (or rather, anti-supernatural) a system for all the intellectual, moral, and even material life of the peoples wise enough to hold to it.

Religion has no obligation. From the moment when the purely human reasoning of the first sages applied itself to knowing the Essence and the Way of all beings, and deduced from it symbols and rites, it is impossible to force people to believe and practice it. That which came out of a human brain is not *a priori* obligatory for other human brains. The most revered masters sought to illuminate the traditional dogmas with the brightest and clearest light; but he who cannot understand is not devalued thereby, nor he who has no time to try to understand. These, along with the most learned and studious men of letters, are still involved in the general evolution, which fortunately they cannot escape, by the very fact of their existence.

Religion has no sanction. It is only in the name of a God, more or less logically invoked, that men can threaten their fellows with punishments and reprisals if they are not believed in all that they say, however incomprehensible. For these threats to be effective, those men must declare themselves, and be believed to be, the echoes of an absent and stern God. Here nothing is *held* to be so: each one is simply *invited* to enlighten himself according to his aptitude and means. Whatever the result of such intellectual effort, no punishment either in earthly or in other lives hangs over those who do not follow the traditional teachings in their hearts.

Religion has no exclusivism. It is perfectly licit, so long as the laws are not infringed, to openly practice Taoism, Buddhism, Confucianism, or any other external cult. It is permitted to change religion, or to belong to none: there is no anathema against anyone.

Since Heaven, as the goal of evolution, constitutes the universality of beings, it would retard this evolution (supposing that to be possible) to cast out or condemn a necessary fragment of this universality.

There is no State religion. There is no religion or cult of the State, nor priests employed by it. The state neither protects nor proscribes any cult; proselytism is nonexistent. The study of Religion is pursued by voluntary students under unpaid masters. All the cults remain side by side under the impartial eye of the State, on the sole condition that they stay within the bounds of conscience, that their adepts do not argue, and that through the ambition or turbulence of their representatives, they do not foment troubles in the Empire or rebellion against the law. There is no persecution: the measures taken in the course of history against such new cults were reactions, not attacks.

There is no paid cult. Each sect or creed maintains its own temples and priests according to the number and generosity of its adepts. No one worries about what happens inside these buildings—which is usually nothing at all since the religions are largely metaphysical, and the liturgies not exclusive to any of them. If the State decrees the place and time of Confucian honors in the commemorative pagodas, it is because the ceremonies instituted in honor of Confucius have never been any sort of religion, but a *civil Rite.*

Religion is not even a family affair, at least as concerns those *translations* known as religions, and especially as regards the external cult. Birth, marriage, and death are not religious affairs, precisely because they are natural affairs, and the head of the family is the only priest there. Between the bonze's pagoda and the family hearth there stand the sovereign authority of the father, with all its legal status, and the familial cult of the Ancestors, with its ancient power: images at their own level of Humanity's primordial and general Tradition. Religion is therefore a matter of personal conscience and individual liberty. The principles of traditional philosophy and metaphysics are transmitted in families by their literate members. Nothing transpires beyond the wall of the paternal enclosure, and no one would have the temerity—useless as it would be—to breach the moral barrier that thus protects the independence and dignity of the citizens.

Liturgies require no external sign. The Rites, defined by a series of laws and rules, are part of the political principles of the empire. With religious practice thus reduced to nothing, its theories are merely the object of courteous and good-humored discussions between members of different cults, where no angry looks are exchanged, no pyres kindled.

As for the moral conduct of peoples, which seems to be the immediate and earthly goal of religions, the natural philosopher Confucius takes care of it without any divine intervention. We know how masterfully this gentle scholar has educated his disciples, and how he has conquered the soul of his race, far better than the prophets of Judea and Islam did with theirs, among carnage and malediction.

Fohi, first among men, *crystallized* the Primordial Tradition; Laotseu drew from it a body of doctrine; Confucius, a moral system. Can one say that one of these intellectual heritages, or their amalgam, formed a *Religion* in the Western sense? It is impossible: nothing could be further from the truth. Yet the Far Eastern races have nothing else to link man with God, and there is no land on earth where belief in the Supreme Being is more universal and seems more reasonable than in theirs. Whence comes this apparent contradiction? It comes from the very essence of the Tradition. There is no need for religion to join man to Heaven:* tradition is sufficient. It is the metaphysical thread that always links Humanity to its Essence. Nothing has broken or weakened it, and so it will be for all time. Humanity will never cease to be born, and *if it ceased to be born, it would have become by that very fact That which engendered it.* Here is the cornerstone of the Tradition. The Far Eastern races, protected by the best of laws and the calmest

---

*The word "Heaven" translates the metaphysical character *Thien*, with which ideographic writing represents the total idea that the West calls God.

history, have never lost sight of that cornerstone. A celestial intervention would teach them no more—and for that reason, no such intervention has happened, nor has any sage or emperor seen fit to simulate one. This is why the belief in Heaven is universal, natural, and logical. For the Chinese, to believe in God is to believe in oneself. In those circumstances there are no atheists.

The consequence in daily practice is that, if the Supreme Being is interested in the evolutions of creation and notably of Humanity, it is totally indifferent to whether Humanity concerns itself with it. Hence, there are no sacrifices, no fear, no alms or gifts made in the name of such a fear. The Lord of Heaven crowns this creation that has come out itself, waiting for it to become sufficiently perfect to return to it. That which is the source from which the river is born, and the sea in which it merges and is lost, could not be the enemy of the waves that compose it at any moment of its course. Thus, without denying the imperfections that inevitably follow divisibility, the Far Easterner has an idea of the dignity of himself, his mind, and his concepts due to him through his heavenly continuity, in no way resembling the abasement into which the revealed religions fling the human creature.

Is the absence of a religious ideal in the motives of their actions responsible for the age-old stagnation of the Far Eastern civilizations? None can say. But this absence of religiosity, by suppressing a powerful ferment of discord, has spared their history many a blow. And this lack of sentimentalism, by giving them no practical curiosity about the Beyond, and by focusing their attention and desires on the paternal and nourishing earth, makes them more easily and immediately contented.

In any case, when studying and investigating the Primordial Tradition, one must always keep in mind these two principles that are at the basis of all Far Eastern science: the grandeur of heaven does not necessitate the abasement of man, and the suffering of man is not a necessary element of his evolution.

2

The First Monument of Knowledge

It is not only chronological reasoning that leads us to seek the *most ancient* monument of knowledge in the Far East: psychological and logical reasoning causes us to identify its *most exact* monument there.

Since Far Easterners are essentially traditional, the essence of their philosophy must lie in the most ancient books. Written in far-off epochs when man had fewer needs, and when his desires were not so strong as to lead him, unconsciously or otherwise, to obscure the truth, these books had to be the source of all later teachings. The filial piety of the Chinese considered that everything relevant to man was contained *virtually* in those first books, and that they potentially included all answers to all problems. Solutions and explanations necessitated by new sciences had to be present, in seed form, in the ancient laws, and should be developed in an analogous way to the solutions they gave to the sciences of their own time. The conviction of this synthesis, so powerful as to contain in embryo all conceivable efforts of the human spirit, provides the basis and certitude of all Asiatic philosophy, and has developed the analogical and deductive way of thinking of the Far Eastern peoples.

This state of mind venerates the institutions and doctrines of the past, to the point of subordinating present actions and future speculations to them. It is also a way of honoring, down to his earliest fragment, the common Ancestor from whom the race arose. This would have two consequences: first, to preserve through all vicissitudes the most ancient books, in all their integrity and with perfect fidelity; second, to prevent divisions of opinion and quarrels between systems, and to create in a single stream of teaching a single school, following the same author and applying all the ingenious tenacity of the race, through the same methods, to the same end. This dual goal was achieved—and we will see with what consequences for the intellectual, historical, and political life of the race.

The first book of China, which is also by far the earliest book in the world, goes back to the emperor Fohi, first sovereign of the historical cycle of the Yellow Race. Although haloed by legends and by a naive and popular respect, its existence is neither contested nor contestable. Fohi reigned over what was then called China from the year 3468 before the Christian era. As mentioned, this chronology is not based on more or less imaginary modern calculations, but on the precise description of the state of the heavens at the epoch of Fohi's reign.*

We should add that the doctrines that passed to posterity under Fohi's name should not be attributed to him personally. Like all the sovereigns of that far-off epoch, Fohi was a savant, a magus, the head of a school; it was even for this very reason that he was chosen as sovereign by his race (the Chinese not having hereditary dynasties until after 2199 BCE). He had friends, disciples, and ministers. All of them made commentaries and interpretations of Fohi's doctrines, which indeed the imperial hexagrams needed—and all this baggage, amalgamated and fused, became the "Doctrine of Fohi." *Fohi* is, as it were, the business name of a metaphysical school, and of several centuries of human thought.

---

*The Chinese have this in common with the Egyptians, the Hindus, and all peoples who are guardians of a Tradition and wish to preserve a serious chronology of it.

Fohi's oeuvre consists of three treatises. Two of them are lost; contemporary writings only mention their titles: the *Lienshan* (Mountain Ranges), or the "Book of Unalterable Principles, against Which Nothing Can Prevail"; and the *Koueitsang* (Return), or the "Book to Which All Questions Should Be Referred to Find Their Solution."

The third treatise, which is the "*first monument of human knowledge*," has the title of *Yiking* (Changes in Circular Revolution). This title recalls that all the apparent modalities of the creator in creation are studied in sixty-four symbols (the hexagrams), *forming a circle*, the last being intimately related to the first. (This is the first occasion to mention that in the Far East, a design is often used in place of a word, so as to allow a specific idea all its synthetic breadth.)

We must add that there were doubtless written monuments before the treatises of which the *Yiking* is the third. These monuments were written, drawn, or carved on the "Roof of the World," the unique cradle of humanity, with the help of signs that all humanity understood, before it was divided by various migrations and thus lost the awareness of its totality. What this unique writing was, we will surely never know except through approximations. A paleographer will never reconstruct a whole script by means of a fragment, as [Georges] Cuvier reconstructed a mammoth from the evidence of one leg. But it was from this unique writing that both the Chinese hierograms and the Chaldean (or Sumero-Akkadian) hieroglyphs descended, at the same epochs and through parallel deformations. It is still possible to determine the influences—quite physical—that caused these deformations.

On this range of the Pamir, which was our common cradle, there reigned a single language and a single script, both of them lost. The day came, either through a cataclysm that brought down the cold that reigns on those heights today, or because the human race, leaning over the rocky edge of its plateaus, felt the vertiginous lure of unknown plains—the day came when men descended to the lower levels by way of the rivers that originate in the primordial plateaus. Those of the South, the future Red race, came by the Dzangbo [Tsangpo] and the Sindh [Indus]; those of the West, the future White race, by the Syr [Syr Darya / Jaxartes] and the Amou [Amu Darya / Oxus]; those of the East, the future Yellow race, by the Hoangho [Yellow] and the Yangtze. Without a backward glance, they all left the ancestral mountain that was the navel of the world. Among them, the ancients and the learned carried Wisdom and the Tradition.

Then on the fertile riverbanks, beneath the warm and kindly sun of the Far East, the Eastern peoples gradually formed their polity. They found there the *bac-chi* (*cay gio, phaong-moc*), from whose fibers they made a fine and supple paper, and brushes softer than silk: marvelous instruments in the agile fingers of their craftsmen. By these subtle means of transmission, the primitive lineaments took the shape of drawings decorated with filled and empty spaces, under the light brush and the dexterous hand.

Meanwhile on the tortuous spaces to the west of the Thianshan [Tien Shan], beneath the devouring Mesopotamian sun, other peoples found on the surface of the ground granites, diorites, marbles—brilliant and hard stones. Heaped up in ramparts, resting on almost indestructible foundations, these formed the monuments of Chaldean power and science. Then, seizing the hammer, these Eastern peoples carved the primitive characters with the help of steel points. Chiseled on the marble surface, these formed constellations of acute triangles, set in straight lines.

These differences, at first due only to the graphic difficulties met with in nature, soon entered into the essence of the hieroglyphs. As the civilizations diverged, the characters through successive deformations became different scripts. Nonetheless, the essential character of the representations remains the same. The synthetic mind reconstitutes the primitive type and discovers, under the veil of the most diverse appearances, the same hieroglyphic sign, luminous and triumphant.

Fohi knew that the hierograms of the thirty-fifth century BCE were only deformations of the primitive script, and thus inadequate for representing abstract and general thoughts. This is precisely the reason that he used the linear symbols of the *Trigrams* to fix the Tradition in the only adequate way, namely synthetic and universal.

The writing of the *Yiking* is of two kinds: the *trigram*, for Fohi's actual text; and the *hierogram* (primitive character or *Koteou*), for the glosses and paraphrases of the School of Fohi.

The basis of the *Yiking* thus consists of sixty-four hexagrams, or double trigrams. These sixty-four types derive from eight trigrams in two concentric circles, rotating in opposite directions. These trigrams in turn derive from four digrams, and the digrams from different positions of the unbroken line — and the broken line – –.

These two types of line are symbolic figures representing the simplest things that could ever be. Whence did Fohi derive such a naive symbolism? Here as elsewhere, both for writing as translation of thoughts and for the thoughts themselves, he did not consult celestial interventions or invisible powers, but simply the nature that surrounded him and enchanted his people. With unarguable logic, he adapted to the human scale the Tradition that was to enlighten and guide humanity. According to the historic book of the *Rites of Tseou*, "Before tracing the trigrams, Fohi looked up to the heavens, then down to the earth, and observed their particularities; he considered the characteristics of the human body and of all external things." That is to say, the two lines indicated a double state, or rather the equality of two states common to all creation. We can compare this straight-lined symbol to the circular one known to all oriental antiquity and revived by the Taoists: the *Yin-yang* representing the double principle—active-passive, male-female, light-dark, positive-negative, et cetera—which, when divided into two parts by analytic observers, produces the fatal error of Good and Evil. Indissolubly one in essence (although material representation is forced to show it otherwise) it constitutes the *Taiky* or *Great Extreme*: the powerful and ultimate symbol carved on the front of all the Temples, and which Laotseu placed at the summit of all Asiatic doctrines.

The unbroken line represents the active; the broken line, the passive. In the lines as in the principles, Fohi recognized the essence and unity of perfection, of which they are only aspects. Here, more than anywhere else in the world, we must beware of confusing the thing with the degraded form that is the only way we can behold or even comprehend it. For the worst metaphysical errors and the worst moral cataclysms have arisen from the misunderstanding and misinterpretation of symbols. Let us always remember the god Janus, who is represented with two faces yet who only has one, which is neither of those that we can touch or see.

Such is the symbolism of the lines of Fohi's hexagrams. It shows clearly that the *Yiking* is a universal book, not a treatise on astronomy as the Japanese and their Latin imitators claim.*

The hierograms that constitute the glosses and paraphrases of the School of Fohi (the chief ones being the "formulae" of Wenwang) are written in primitive characters called *Koteou*. These characters are the origin of the "keys" that exist, to this day, in Chinese ideographic writing. Among the documents of the Far East we no longer have the actual script of the School of Fohi. We might question its value and its forms, for it no longer survives in brush-written manuscripts, had it not resisted ages and revolutions like the rock in which it was carved. The hierograms in question are to be found in the famous inscription of

---

*Although Monsieur Philastre's opinion is somewhat similar, we take the opportunity to recommend his translation of the *Yiking*, which is unique because of his knowledge of Chinese characters—and of the Chinese character. The deep cause that gave Philastre an immense erudition also ruined his diplomatic career (*Annales du Musee Guimet*, vols. VIII and XXIII). [Paul-Louis-Félix Philastre (1837–1902); see below, pp. 172–73, for Matgioi's remarks on Philastre's work and career. —*Trans.*]

Yu on the mountain of Heng-Chan [Heng Shang Nan] and preserved at Singan-fou [Sianfu/Xi'an], the first capital of historic China. That town remains not only the most epic souvenir of Chinese antiquity, but at the present hour is still the sacred refuge that victoriously shelters the sovereigns of modern China against the warlike attempts of a European coalition.

Aside from its sculptural value, this inscription is too interesting for us not to quote at least part of it. It is in fact contemporary with the Hebrew flood, which it mentions. It goes back to precisely 2276 BCE, which is five centuries before the oldest Egyptian hieroglyphics:

> Comfort me, my counselors, in the administration of affairs. In the West and beyond the mountains the greater and lesser isles, the peopled plateaus, the dwellings of birds and beasts are flooded far and wide. Take note of this: Make the waters flow, raise dikes to prevent another overflow.

And further on:

> For a long time I have completely neglected my people, so as to repair the damage of the flood. But now I can rest: The confusion of nature has ceased; the great currents that came from the South have flowed into the sea.

We have long known that the biblical Flood was a partial inundation and a comparatively minor cataclysm, but each one judges events according to the good or ill that it does him. Emperor Yu saw only a provincial inundation, whereas the Hebrew historian saw the destruction of nature and, consequently, the finger of his Jehovah. A few dikes would suffice to prevent a similar disaster, and so it is the Minister of Public Works who here replaces the dove of Noah's Ark. Once again, Yu's inscription advises us not to take literally the grandiloquent claims of little nations, and to remind us, for example, that in the twenty-second century BCE it didn't take much water to drown the Jewish race and its power.*

The glosses that accompany Fohi's hexagrams, all of them now transcribed in modern ideographic script, comprise the formulae of Prince Wenwang, founder of the Tsheou [Zhou] Dynasty (1154 BCE); the formulae of Tsheou Kong (1122 BCE); the "Twelve Wing-beats" of Kongtzeu (Confucius, ca. 500 BCE); the "Traditional Commentary" of Tchengtze (ca. 1150 CE), and the *primitive meaning* of the famous Tsouhi [Zhu Xi] (1182 CE). Each of these commentators explains the text of Fohi and Wenwang according to his own lights. And since this text is synthetic and universal, we will see in turn its metaphysical, political, magical, moral, social, or divinatory meaning, according to the leanings of its interpreters.

Their tranquil audacity matches the simplicity of their reasoning. Recall that Fohi and Wenwang—especially Fohi—considered themselves as translators of the Eternal Word, without having to imagine a divine intermediary between that Word and themselves.

That is why the *Yiking*, which we will begin to analyze directly, opens with the *tangible* study of Unity and Perfection, namely, the human study of heaven. And it is not for love of paradox, but of veracity, that we begin the next section with the *"Graphics of God."*

There is no doubt that the meaning of the formula is wrapped in obscurity, largely due to the synthetic habit of Chinese reasoning and the ideogrammatic character of their writing. As Philastre says:

A Chinese character never has an absolutely defined and limited meaning. The meaning derives from its position in the phrase, and

---

*The Emperor Yu's inscription contains something very different if we know how to read it as it should be read, on three successive levels. We will return to this in a special article, where we will analyze, apart from these remarks on the biblical Deluge, the instructions of the Emperor Yu to his counselors and disciples, in the three worlds.

also from its use in "some book or other" and from the interpretation admissible in that case. The word has no value apart from its traditional acceptances.

Moreover, the obscurity of the text and commentaries appears intentional, to give parallel and equally valid meanings to the same group of characters, which can be read in as many ways as there are degrees in understanding, sciences in humanity, and worlds in the intellectual universe. We recognize from these specific characters that the *Yiking* is indeed "*The Book*" without further epithet. It is both synthetic and abstract, logical and divinatory, political and metaphysical, ontological and moral, and the Chinese schools were right to consult and cite it under all these aspects.

The path of studying Chinese philosophies is not mapped out like that of Western philosophies, and it is impossible to disengage Chinese thought from a certain ambiguity. Our intelligence sees this ambiguity not as intentional but as troubling, showing an incapacity for reasoning. Nothing could be more mistaken. Oriental science differs from our own not only due to race and country, but also to epoch. One should not expect to find in Fohi's descendants and Laotseu's contemporaries those clear and straightforward statements of which we are so proud: statements that are indeed correct, but through being narrow and strict contain only a minimal part of the truth. All these tiny portions, affirmed singly and independently of each other by our analytic minds, hide the whole truth from our weak and myopic eyes. That is how a face would appear, grossly distorted, in a mirror cut into a thousand facets juxtaposed on different planes. Microscopic discussions have made us unable to appreciate and grasp the larger syntheses.

I would compare the situation of a Westerner transported to China to that of a peasant of the plains, suddenly lifted to the top of Mont Blanc. His senses, unaccustomed to the depths and distant horizons, and the unfamiliar shudder of vertigo would prevent him from enjoying the splendor of the landscape. That is the kind of discomfiting feeling we have when faced with the Chinese systems and modes of reasoning. Ill-prepared as we are through want of familiarity, this immutable order regulating the universe seems to us nothing but a complicated theory, in whose spaces and depths our unperceptive minds become impatient, resistant, and distracted before they have understood it.

One who seeks initiation into the Primordial Tradition, which offers us the first monument of knowledge, must be warned: he will feel a vague and uncanny sense of disquiet, not only because of its universality but also because of the generality of the terms used, the forced impropriety of the interpretations, and the Westerner's total lack of preparation for reading and writing in an analytic language whose perfect sense and whole meaning resides only in the ideograms. One who wants to penetrate deeply into this science and this thought must seek the necessary help and clarity in the original books, not in a scholastic summary, and still less in a foreign adaptation. This is the great fault of works by the most distinguished Sinologists like Stanislas Julien and many others. A long sojourn in China, among Chinese literary people, would unquestionably have given them the solutions that they sought in vain in fruitless labors at the Sorbonne or the Collège de France. It was a very long sojourn that facilitated Philastre's work on the *Yiking*. It was living in the Far East that would have allowed missionaries like Fathers [Evariste Régis] Huc and [Joseph Henri Marie] de Prémare to plumb the meaning of the obscurest arcana, if the Roman religious idea within which they worked had not given them a one-track mind and forced them to draw absurd conclusions from their work, which would not have occurred to them for a moment if their profession had not made it an unavoidable necessity.

For these reasons and under these conditions, it is impossible to explain the *Yiking* other than via the Far Eastern philosophers and their arguments. Next, one must understand how to obtain and apply this aid. Not like the Western commentators, who with strict formulae and imperturbable deductions have illuminated all the fine aspects of the Greek genius, for example, precisely because the Greek genius, from which that of the Latin races emerged, perfectly suits our methods of intellectual argument and dissection. For the same reason that the Chinese genius seems on first sight vague and abstruse, under such methods the vast Chinese synthesis would not be analyzed and illuminated, but fragmented and destroyed, leaving us with nothing but a bruised and crumpled corpse. Using one book to explain another should not be taken in an absolute manner, either for its ideas or its terminology. To explain a text by a context would here be the height of naivety, and also of error. There is only one valid way to explain one Oriental text by another, and to present their thought in symbolic form. It is to immerse oneself deeply in a philosopher's teaching—that of Laotseu, for example—and absorb his manner of using the terms of the Ancient Study. Then, when faced with a confused text with multiple interpretations from one of the archaic *Kings*, one intuits the way that Laotseu would have understood it. The texts seem divergent but are only different. They all tend toward the one truth, just as the waves of the sea, seemingly varying in height, color, and direction, are all going the same way under the constant influence of winds and tides.

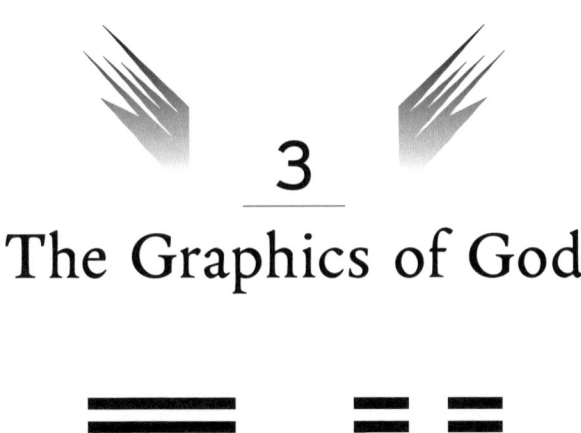

3

The Graphics of God

Like a child, who is better taught to swim by suddenly throwing him into the water than by holding him up with lifebelts and lessons from experts, it is better to plunge into the sacred metaphysics of the Far East, even at the risk of sometimes losing our foothold there. After some surprise and much attention, any thoughtful and sensible mind will find its way.

There is a primordial and absolute difference between the Western and Eastern concepts of God, the origin of the Gods, and the idea of God. In the West our alphabetic languages give our object of study the four-lettered name *Dieu*, which is so marvelously concrete and precise that its limitations are all too obvious. Unsatisfied even with this designation, Westerners picture him as an old man with a beard and a handful of lightning-bolts, or by a triangle with an eye in the middle. Here in the East, what we call God has no name; it is represented by a character called Thien, which spoken Mandarin translates as "heaven." This character assumes and includes a number of properties that are not special to heaven, but to what is *in* heaven or *beyond* it. Thus, the God of the Far Eastern peoples is not called by a proper name: it is a general idea. However, Fohi, China's first historic magus, judged that this "general idea" was totally inadequate, incorrect, and a source of error. He replaced the character with a geometric design, unspecific and as generic as possible, whose form would represent the reasonings by which one might approach an inconceivable idea. Thus, this geometric design takes on the value of a metaphysical arcanum.

The Westerner's ambition is to be understood; that of the Oriental is to be true. These two ambitions exclude one another in theogony, in metaphysics, and in every transcendent science. We cannot grasp the truth unless it is surrounded and wrapped up, as it were, with errors. Our task is always to distinguish this error, unconscious and necessary, from the truth that it harbors. It is also to lessen its denseness and quantity, so that as this envelope becomes ever thinner, the truth can at last break through.

It was in this spirit that the Far Eastern Magi constructed the Graphics of God, which carry the generic determinant of "Perfection." They count two perfections (hence, two graphics of God): active perfection and passive perfection.* But in reality there is only one perfection—and we will next clear Chinese metaphysics of the reproach of dualism that uninformed minds make at this point.

There is only a single perfection, a single idea of God, a single "initial cause of all things." This perfection, called "active," is the generator and potential reservoir of all *activity*, but it does not in the least *act*. It is, and remains in itself, without any possible manifestation. Thus, it is unintelligible to man, in the present state of the human compound.

When this perfection has manifested itself, without ceasing to be

---

*Khien and Khouen: these two generalizing terms are used to represent the idea of God. We will continue to render it by "Perfection"—an inferior term, but we are loath to encumber transcendental metaphysics with a new terminology, being aware that terminologies are the subject of arguments, errors, and disrepute. Those who create them for the supposed needs of their demonstrations make their texts bristle incomprehensibly. They become so enamored of them that these arid and useless terminologies often end up as the only novelty of the proposed system.

itself it has undergone the modification* that makes it intelligible to the human mind. It matters little whether this manifestation is a simple act of will, or a veritable action. By the very fact that perfection has acted, it is fit to enter into conceptuality and is then called "passive perfection" (Khouen). Perfection is one, and unintelligible to man. In order to speak of it, it must become intelligible, or at least one must suppose that it can. Thus, it is represented by two different graphics. But there is still only one sole and unique perfection, and a single initial cause.

Let us not forget that our mind can only grasp number; it is not able to grasp Unity, and still less the Zero, which is the unity before all manifestation. Let us also remember that one can only speak of dualism when there are two contrary or different principles, and that two (or a hundred) aspects of a single principle constitute neither dualism nor multiplicity. Here, as everywhere, the Great Principle is one, and it is in order to situate its nonmanifested unity above all possible efforts of human intelligence that the sage offers for our contemplation and study not the principle in itself (which cannot be named without being disfigured), but the aspect of the Great Principle that is manifested and reflected in human consciousness.

I am obliged to insist on this, almost to excess, and I will do so again for the Yin-yang, or symbol of the Great Extreme. For it is astonishing and almost ridiculous to see excellent minds reproaching a metaphysical system, or an occult tradition, for a dualism that has only been introduced into it by the current imperfection of human mentality, and to make it approachable by that mentality. There is indeed a reproach to be made: but those excellent minds should address it to themselves, scolding themselves for still remaining human. We must be resigned to the fact that, as humans, we will never know the truth—and that

---

*[Matgioi's use of the word *modification* (the same in French and English) has been retained throughout, despite some clumsiness of diction. Its virtue in such phrases as the "human modification" is a reminder that the state or class in question is not an independent entity, but a manifestation, however limited, of Perfection. —*Trans.*]

what we believe to be the truth is not the truth, for the very reason that we understand what it is or may be.* It is, therefore, with infinite precaution that the Tradition includes an aspect of the truth—or of God—capable of being grasped by our intelligence. And in order that this aspect should not be spoken (and thus give rise to a false statement or misleading interpretations), this aspect is not a character, nor even an idea: it is a drawing. Such is the linear and metaphysical arcanum of Passive Perfection (Khouen).

To go to the bottom of this question once and for all, this aspect is not a reflection. Passive perfection is not a reflection of active perfection, like the reflection of a star in water, in other words, half of a fiction. Passive Perfection is absolutely an entity, an entity identical (or rather, which must be identical) to the entity of active Perfection, except for this one circumstance: that we can approach it. In other words, active Perfection, grasped by our imperfect understanding, becomes passive Perfection. Yet it remains Perfection, and therein bursts forth its mysterious abstract reality.

If we transpose numeric truth to the divine level (or transcendental metaphysics), we can say that passive Perfection is to active Perfection as the number *one* is to *zero*—which, although different *numerals*, are but a single *number*, both the first of numbers and the *only number*.

One cannot contest too strongly this instinctive and formidable error of the human mind that projects this multiplicity onto the Truth, being unable to comprehend it otherwise: a unique example in the whole mental universe, which through unconscious pride projects its mental imperfection onto the very face of divinity. This dualism is at the basis of all metaphysical errors. The human mind forgets to consider the necessary juxtaposition of two absolutely identical

---

*For if the truth is perfect and if we have the truth, we participate in perfection, and we are gods, which seems an absurd supposition. Or else, if we are imperfect and if we possess the truth, the truth is not at all perfect—and this supposition is truly absurd.

principles (necessary, so that by comprehending the existence of the second it can admit the existence of the first, without having to comprehend it). The human mind, tending to divide and differentiate, soon assigns to these juxtaposed principles different properties, then dissimilar appearances, followed by contrary directions, and ends up making them enemies of one another. Then the damage is done. It is irreparable and poisons the very roots of sciences and religions. And there is worse: Man, who cannot long remain a metaphysician, a logician, and a reasoner, quickly becomes sentimental, sensitive, and sensual. Into this new domain he drags the error that he created on the mental plane, which is his fault alone. And on this lower plane he creates the monstrous image of his metaphysical dualism: the relative qualities of Good and Evil. He draws up laws, installs conventions, and makes himself a martyr by his prejudices, consolidating his detestable work with the blood and tears that he has caused to be shed. He then places this moral dualism under the protection of the metaphysical dualism invented by his ignorance and pride. Finally, as warden of his own prison, he constructs with his own illogical hands the incomprehensible, stupid, and lie-ridden hell that is the social aggregate of today.

The graphic representation of Perfection, as shown at the head of this chapter, is conceived from the simplest possible symbolism. The *drawing* of the infinite idea, being indefinite, cannot be better shown than as an element without beginning or end: hence it is a straight line that can extend indefinitely in either direction. Of course, when it is drawn, material necessity makes it stop short, but in thought or imagination it never ends. This is why, despite appearances, the symbolism of the straight line is superior to that of the curved, closed line, or of the circumference. That resembles the serpent biting its tail, a popular and misleading image of Eternity. By circling indefinitely around itself, it seems endless. But in reality, and to be precise, it encloses a space and defines a surface, which is the circle—and that has a dimension, hence it is finite. Nothing can prevent this determination, which explains the inferiority and manifest inadequacy of this symbol.

With the straight line, on the contrary, the more one imagines it perpetually prolonged, the more it is *depersonalized*, making it the proper image of the *indefinite*, since it does not determine, does not clasp, *does not define anything*. Better yet, if I imagine any plane engendered by this line, I have the indefinity of space. And if I imagine simultaneously *all* the planes engendered by this indefinite line, I have the *"universal volume,"* the symbol of the infinite. That is the reason, almost always misunderstood, why the straight line is superior to the circumference as a symbolic representation.

If we now think of Perfection—in other words, if our thought makes passive Perfection out of active Perfection—we will recognize the absolute identity of these entities, both in depth and in form. Then, by the very fact of thinking, we join to passive perfection the idea of our multiplicity and our divisibility (the special character of the human modification and of thought, which is special to the human state).

Thus, the symbol of passive perfection must be at every point the symbol of active perfection and must also engender the idea of multiplicity (the determinate *"more"* being metaphysically a *"less"*). That is why the symbol of passive Perfection will be the indefinite straight line, with an indefinite series of interruptions of its continuity. Such is the significance of the broken line from the point of view of the divisibility of Being, namely, the point of view of the multiplicity of actions and forms. Thus, we possess two symbols that are true, powerful, and simple. Upon these are built the trigrams of Fohi, the hexagrams of the *Yiking*, and the sixty-four arcana of Evolution.

As we have already said, active Perfection does not act, but is "pregnant" with all action, and *from the human point of view*, the *action principle* is the proof of its perfection, and the beginning of the possibility of its intellection. This why the Chinese magus, addressing human beings and wishing them to understand the highest human level of Metaphysics, put in first place *activity*.* And the supreme mark of activity, for its perfection, is the power to *perfectly engender*, that is, to reproduce itself without assistance. This very natural idea (which, without the slightest wordplay, can be called the *mother idea*) translates into graphic symbolism by doubling the sign of perfection (active or passive, continuous or broken line) with a similar line. Thus, the digram is formed. This digram is the precise symbolic representation of the Father and the Mother, the means of conception—and so the two lines conceive the third. As the Father and the Mother engender the child, in symbolism the trigram immediately emerges from the digram, which is not a permanent state but a *passage* from Unity to the Triad. Such is the genesis of Fohi's trigrams.

We emphasize the fact that the state of the digram lasts only an instant, for its profound metaphysical and moral consequences. In the whole formidable work of the *Yiking* and all its commentaries, the digram's existence is mentioned only once, worth about one printed line in Western letters. This intentional silence shows that it is not a logical state, but merely a necessary instant between Unity and Trinity. The Father alone counts as existent, and the eternal androgyne only separates to fecundate itself. And the instant is *mathematical*; the father and mother exist only to create. At the moment of creation, they are united and form only one. The moment they separate, the germ exists, and they are already three.† It may be interesting to apply this principle in every sphere. For instance, there is no good or evil outside human relativity; there is no union of soul and body without the spirit; in Catholic and Kabbalistic terms, there is no Father and Son without the Holy Spirit—the Christian mystery of the Trinity

---

*The character Khien, which represents Perfection ideogrammatically, is translated into language as the *Activity of Heaven*.
†In practice, the Far Easterner calculates his age by adding ten months before the day of his birth.

becomes an axiom, and the societies and religions that ignore the Word of St. John and the Paraclete are nothing but illogical and monstrous aggregations. We leave our readers, who are evidently well informed on all these questions, with the facile but dubious pleasure of drawing all the deductions that this metaphysical theorem implies.

The trigrams made from the same sorts of line are naturally those of Perfection. By combining the straight and broken line in all possible positions we get eight trigrams, which are the "Trigrams of Fohi" and the basis of all the metaphysical symbolism of the Far Eastern peoples.

From these trigrams emerge the hexagrams that make up the basis of the *Yiking*. Practically, or one might say, mechanically, they "evolve" from one to another. By doubling the initial trigrams—writing them twice, one above the other, and inscribing them as one inscribes an octagon in a circle—one obtains the magical table popularly known as *Hado*. If one rotates the outer circle of trigrams from left to right, and simultaneously rotates the inner circle from right to left around the common center, one obtains sixty-four situations of the six lines, all different, which make up the sixty-four arcana of Evolution. The sixty-fifth would be identical to the first, reproducing the two hexagrams of Perfection. The *Yiking* consists precisely of the explanation, formulae, and commentaries on this series, justifying its title—even graphically—of "*Changes in circular revolution*," and at the same time symbolizing the fundamental dogma of the Far Eastern Tradition in all its modifications and its final transformation. We will later develop this symbolism, so simple and so perfect.

There is a profound reason for doubling the trigrams and converting them to hexagrams, a reason both human and metaphysical, and familiar to all. The trigram—or, more generally, the ternary idea that it represents—is the image of a metaphysical entity that really exists, but at an infinite distance from humanity, far beyond and above our intellectual horizon. It is reflected in our understanding as an object is reflected in the water that bathes its base, or out at sea, the moon reflected as it sets in the ocean. Just so, the celestial trigram and its reflection in our reason produce the hexagram. The ternary principle shines through again here, for heaven is not reflected on earth except through the human heart. The monument is only reflected in the water thanks to the light of day; the soul does not influence the body except through the mediation of the Spirit. The Son only communicates the Father's grace, and the Father only distributes the Son's merits, by virtue of the Holy Spirit. *Three* make *one*, through the effect of a fugitive and latent *two*. And the hexagram is an *enneagram* of which the celestial trigram is real, the human trigram a reflection, and the spiritual trigram is inscribed in a medium so tenuous and fluid that it leaves no trace, no witness—logic alone indicates the necessity of its existence.

One may have noticed by now, and will notice more in what follows, how many universal thoughts the Far Eastern tradition has given birth to, for all its distance and remoteness. At every moment of these studies, which seem more forbidding than they really are, their applicability to our own methods and our Western traditions will emerge clearly and indubitably—traditions that centuries of White civilization have transformed while thinking it was improving or purging them. It will be a great help for understanding the doctrine, and a strong reassurance to the synthetic minds whom we want to reach, to see that the link is not broken and never can be. It joins us to the common origin from which we come just as much as Fohi himself came, and to which we return just as much as Fohi's most respectful followers. We have nothing to create, nothing to invent or even to explain with new methods. We have only not to lose what is left to us, and to recover what we have mislaid. And let us speak out loud here what all the metaphysicians and occultists of every land have quietly thought and known. In the obscuration and oblivion of the sacred sciences, there is a question of race and latitude. The wise men of China and India have forgotten nothing, whereas we have been separated from them by barbarians. It is only the Ninevites, destroyers of the Vedic sciences, and the Semites, inadequate and cruel copyists of the Egyptian sciences, who have created a hiatus between antiquity and the present, between Oriental science and Western learning. We will regain our path by passing beside, across, or over those mediocre races, and reattaching modern humanity worthily to its ancestors of the cycle of Ram.* If the sequel to these studies succeeds in proving these propositions to a wider public, we will have started our work in the best way.

But for now, after this simple definition of the *"Graphics of God,"* let us say how admirable is the science that we are pursuing, how simple the method we are using! We have declared the God-Being, or Perfection, unintelligible to man. And so it is in reality. We have stated how the religious systems revered by most of humanity try to disfigure God, bringing it closer to us so that our understanding can penetrate it. These systems deliberately destroy the metaphysical idea, thus offering us more than just an error. By establishing anthropomorphism, they present us with a thesis as crude as the fetishism of the uncivilized races. And despite these deformations, they do not satisfy us in the slightest.

As followers of the Primordial Tradition, we have not wanted to—nor could we have—imitated these belittling transformations. God—Perfection—remains to us, and will remain unintelligible as long as we remain human. But this perfection that we could not comprehend, discuss, rationalize, or name, we have *drawn* it—and in drawing it, *we have given it no contours*; we have not *completed* it, yet we know it with our eyes. Through a sequence of logical and metaphysical reasonings, without having established a single proposition *a priori*, required acceptance of a single *postulate*, nor imposed belief in the slightest mystery, we have symbolized perfectly in six lines, without destroying or lessening it, this notion of God that none but God itself could ever name and comprehend. We feel deeply that this simple trace, this linear

---

*[Reference to Fabre d'Olivet's system of prehistory, in which Ram (or Rama) instituted the first universal empire. —*Trans.*]

abstraction, this metaphysical arcanum is as presented here, and cannot be otherwise. And we hold in our hand this marvelous instrument, by which we can confidently present the ideal, complete, and axiomatic representation of the unintelligible. We do not comprehend it; we do not name it; we do not write it. We see it.

And it is this symbol, more admirable than the most magnificent ideas the human brain can conceive, that will be the basis and starting point of all our propositions, just as what it represents is the unmissable goal of our existence and our efforts.

4

The Symbols of the Word

As we have already said, the spirit of generalization has remained intact among the Eastern races—that spirit of generalization in which all of humanity philosophized before the invention of analyses and methods of dissection by the modern spirit of applied and mechanical science. The oldest traditional books are rooted in the synthetic, mathematical, and logical method, which the reverence of their guardian peoples has transmitted, uncorrupted and inviolable, right up to our extremely civilized and individualistic times.

This generalizing spirit applies the same axiom or principle in countless cases: it applies it to all sciences, all social states, all intellectual worlds, and to everything that can be done, spoken, or thought in all places and epochs of the human and universal state.

These applications are ardently sought and precisely determined, and all the more when an axiom seems fundamental, and a principle seems timelessly conceived and correct in its graphic symbol.

Thus, the *"Graphics of God,"* established with a view to universal synthesis in thought and mathematical rigor in execution, are considered by the commentators on the Traditional Books to be the key to all human ideas and situations. They saw them as the beginning and end of all sciences; as the arcanum where one should seek the explanation of every unknown, the general solution of all problems, the rules of all politics, the prescriptions for all social economies and all individual morals.

Consequently, the *"Graphics of God"* are in practice not merely the perfect "Design" of a general, abstract idea, and of an entity inconceivable to man today. With their six indefinite lines, they are like a metaphysical musical staff on which the eternal harmony is written and the particular chords of each piece of human knowledge are placed, in order to have their proper significance in the concert of the universe. To use an easier and cruder comparison, though still accurate from the graphic point of view, each piece of human knowledge is like one of those diplomatic communications full of superfluous ramblings intended to mislead and distract the ignorant and the indiscreet, but in which lies the solution of problems on which the life and glory of nations depends. If they fall into ignorant hands, these letters remain incomprehensible—they only make sense to their writers and the intended recipients. Thus, human knowledge as a whole is abstruse even to those who studied it deeply, if they pursued individual studies and specialized in their efforts.

The *"Graphics of God"* are the "grid" placed over the formless text to extract the useful portions and eliminate the inert ones. Its gaps, *always in the same arrangement, no matter what the text*, bring to light for knowing eyes the essential truths, the ruling arcana of all sciences, and the driving forces of all human actions.

Now let us enter straight into Far Eastern symbolism. The *Graphics of God* will greatly help us if we know how to relate everything to this principle, and if we remember that all interpretations, images, and precise definitions are but embroideries sprinkled on this eternal fabric, this metaphysical loom without which no stuff could be woven, no system could stand.

By combining the "situations" of the *Graphics of God* with one another, and studying the component lines, first individually then in parallel, one obtains all the ideas of the brain and every light of consciousness. As one applies them, these situations are modified, these lines change their personifications and their objects. A perpetual movement arises in and between them, the result of the primordial activity and the consequence of the potential activity of Perfection. This ceaseless motion perfectly represents the series of transformative modalities that, one after another, make up the existence of the tangible and perceptible universe: modalities whose tetragrammatic formula (to be studied in the next chapter) gives their deep cause and formal explanation. Thus, each of the ideograms and each of their lines, participating in the Principle of Activity, possesses its own activity by which it moves freely, conforming to the freely accepted path of which it is one of the expressions (and the only immediate expression at the moment one speaks of it).

The result is that each of the lines, so long as one considers it, takes on a personality due to the manifestation of its particular activity. It seems logical and sensible that the intellectual and phonetic symbolism (we will soon understand the reason for pairing these adjectives) has given them the express figure of All Power and All Activity, namely that of the DRAGON, "omniscient master of the right and left paths" (*Phan-Khoatu*, I).

The Legend of the Dragon. "Dragons and fish have the same origin, but how different their destinies! The fish cannot live outside its element, but the moment a light cloud descends toward the earth, we see the dragon leaping into the air." Thus sings the eleventh verse of the famous ballad *The Joyous Life*, at the sound of which, throughout the Far East, old scholars smile and infants fall asleep.

It alludes to the legend of the Dragon, which we will quote because one will find there the origin of the Mosaic Genesis, the Sinaitic fiction of the law, and perhaps also the symbol of alchemical synthesis.

The water that flows on the earth, say the old storytellers, is like the cloud that floats in the sky. There are similar in nature; they only differ in appearance. And that is the important thing, because humidity makes the universe fruitful, just as the way of heaven fertilizes the thoughts of men. Nothing is better, more fugitive, active, and universal, than water. But if their actions are not united, the water of the sky can do nothing on the earth, and the water of the earth can do nothing for the cloud in the sky. Thus, in the earth's water dwells the fish, and in the sky's water the Hac bird,* living separately—and they are imperfect. However, if the storm raises the waters or the heat of the day evaporates them; if a light mist descends on the ground, or a great wind drives the clouds down to earth, then there is union between the two waters, earthly and heavenly. The Hac bird comes down to earth like the clouds, and the fish rises to the sky like the river water. When they meet, the Hac bird lends the fish its wings, and the fish lends the bird its body and its scales. Among thunderclaps and roaring waters the Great Fish appears, on whose back are written the secret precepts of the Law. And as soon as its back has touched the lowered clouds, it becomes the Long Dragon and vanishes in the air with the clouds that cover and sweep it away.

I would not think for a moment of explaining this popular legend, which is clearer than all the Mosaic parables and the Judeo-Christian legend of the apple. The youngest pupils in Far Eastern schools comment on it and strip it of its fable with the greatest of ease. I imagine that it would be an easy game for attentive Western scholars, who will thank me much more for inviting them to a small personal task of analogical appropriation, than to have seemed to insult their intelligence through labored elucidations.

Nonetheless, I will stress a few points worthy of meditation. Heaven and earth are, in reality, only one. They are united, to our eyes, by a universal vehicle, and the Chinese Sage has taken as its symbol what may seem the *subtlest matter*, namely evaporated water. Infinitely subtle yet still material, such is the characteristic of the universal vehicle. Here the Chinese Sage meets the theosophic dogma (not surprisingly, since their doctrines are close sisters) and also the Platonic doctrine,

---

*The symbolic and legendary crane.

the assertions of the Gnostic school, and of St. Clement of Alexandria on the materiality of the human soul.

Let it be clear, too, that "Perfection" only exists through the union of Heaven and Earth, and that it is only in this union that the Dragon manifests—and straightaway vanishes in the air. This symbol is understood in two ways: one is that the universe is always in an extreme state of activity; the other is that Perfection is invisible to human eyes, nor is it intelligible to the human mind. It vanishes if it is seen or comprehended by us—it is no longer Perfection. Thus, the Dragon is a symbol that man imagines, but which does not exist for him. Yet it really exists in the total union, realized thanks to the universal vehicle.

Take now the symbol of the Dragon. While we may find the language childlike, let us keep it as an excellent image, and as a useful abbreviation in metaphysical propositions.

I have said above that it was a perfect "intellectual and phonetic" symbol. The explication of the legend applies to the intellectual; the phonetic is more curious still, and generalizes and explains all the preceding facts. So what does this symbolic Dragon really mean in Far Eastern metaphysics? What is this universal vehicle, that is, as it were, the *Aura* of the symbol? It is nothing other than the *Word*, not only as understood by savants and commentators, but as demonstrated by philology itself.

We know what is meant by the LOGOS of Platonic and Alexandrian philosophy. The radical LOG is pronounced with emphasis and as a long syllable. *This is exactly the name of the ideogram of the Dragon*: it is LONG,* with a long O and the N short and unvoiced. In the viceroyalties of central China, it is pronounced LOGUE with mute E. Thus, philology brings its astonishing witness to metaphysics. There has never

---

*I refer the philologically curious to the actual text of the *Yiking*, found in Philastre's translation (*Annales du Musée Guimet*) and to the graphics and grammars of Père S. Couvreur, S.J., missionary of Tcheou-li, printed at Hokien-fou in 1884, and still quite frequently found in Paris.

been but a single truth; the symbols of this truth differ, but the very pronunciation of its name is everywhere identical. The Platonic Logos and the Word of St. John the Apostle, which the Christians superficially exalt at the end of all their sacrifices,* have no more immediate representation, nor more exact symbolism in all of humanity than this universal and invisible Dragon, which from the height of Heaven covers all the Oriental philosophies with its mysterious shadow.

Khien: The action of Heaven, which is activity. The gifted man imitates it by ceaseless effort. (*Yiking*: traditional Commentary of Tsheng-tse and Confucius on the first hexagram).

The *gifted man*, who is mentioned all through the *Yiking*, and for whose use its precepts were formulated, is an expression unique to the Far Eastern peoples. It would be easy—as others have found—to fill volumes with commentaries on this expression, to define its exact meaning. In other languages one finds Initiates, Magi, High Priests, Free Judges, Saints, the Blessed, Mahatmas, and other terms. In this matter we will keep to the Chinese Tradition's simple and sensible definition. The *gifted man*, it says, is a scholastic term that corresponds to a state of perfection inferior to perfection itself and superior to wisdom. Let us be content with that elastic definition, at least from the point of view of its expression. We imagine that there are several stages in the state of the gifted man and will leave it to circumstances to tell us in each particular case what intellectual and psychic stage he has attained on his path to perfection.

---

*[That is, the opening verses of St. John's Gospel, recited at the end of the Mass. —*Trans.*]

The reason for being, says Tsheng-tse, has no visible form, hence its meaning is explained with an image. As the legend tells it, the Dragon rises in the universal vehicle through the six lines of the Khien, occupying six different positions and giving a meaning to each of these lines as it passes them, exactly as an acoustic series gives a harmonic chord as soon as it is written on a musical staff. The expression of that chord belongs to it alone, but the lines of the staff are its translator and *vehicle.*

There are consequently as many human "staves" as there are hexagrams, namely sixty-four. Let us examine in detail the "passage of the Dragon" through Khien, the hexagram of perfection in itself. It will be an analogical example, well worth following for the metaphysical explication of the other hexagrams, but most importantly it is from this first hexagram that the Chinese magi and philosophers have drawn their principles and their best teachings in all branches of human wisdom.*

The Dragon is "intelligence whose modifications are unlimited, symbol of the transformations of the rational way (*tao*) of the activity expressed by Khien" (*Yiking*, ch. 1, sec. 8, commentary by Tsheng-tse). It rests on the first and lowest line, which is positive because, like all those of the arcanum, its continuity is uninterrupted. It represents "the point of departure of the beginning of beings." It is the "*hidden Dragon.*"

The extreme activity of Perfection is not produced, nor revealed by any act of will or even by any thought. It is thus hidden, meaning unintelligible to man. It is the period of *non-acting.* And by the word "period" we should understand the metaphysical state, just as by the word "situation" we should understand the geometric position, all these conceptions being independent of the relativities of time and space.

---

*At each situation of the Dragon, recall the voyage of the *Légende.* [Probably an allusion to Victor Hugo's epic poem of human destiny, *La Légende des Siècles* (The Legend of the Ages). —*Trans.*]

Placed on the second line, the Dragon emerges: activity begins to make itself felt on the surface of the earth. This is the *"Dragon in the paddy field."* The extreme activity of heaven is not yet manifested, but man senses that it exists, just as a creature in the paddy field is hidden by the rice. One doesn't see it, but one knows it is there because of the waves on the surface made by its passage. Note here that the second line is the *median* line of the lower trigram, hence the résumé, as it were, of its general expression. Note, too, that there is a meaning to be drawn from its comparison with the median line of the upper trigram, which is in sympathy with it (due to the system of correspondences). This meaning gives the general tendency of the hexagram. Since the two corresponding lines are both positive, the meaning of the Khien is *reinforced*, namely, that the activity of heaven is extreme, continuous, eternal, and *Heaven is not conceivable apart from the idea of its activity.* This is what we have already brought out in an earlier chapter—and here as elsewhere, the significances of the symbolic staff of six lines corroborate the metaphysical and the experimental principles already known.

This second situation is summed up perfectly by Shiseng's comparison: "The positive ether begins to engender, just as the sun's light begins to illuminate all things before it appears on the horizon."

Placed on the third line, the Dragon manifests. It is on the higher location of the first trigram, which is the moment in the legend when, rising to the peak of the roaring waters, it prepares to leap up and appear in reality as it is. If the Dragon's scales issue from the water, then man knows science and law. It is the *"visible Dragon."* The incessant activity, arrived at the top of one trigram, mounts into the abyss that separates it from the second trigram. This is a matter for serious circumspection, and we will immediately apply this advice as it is given. There is risk and danger in "seeing the Dragon's back," that is, in knowing the Science and the Law, if one is not sufficiently prepared by previous states. (Compare the Edenic state and the legend of the forbidden fruit.) Here is the *will of all beings for expansion*: it is very perfect because it is the crown of activity, but very dangerous because it may end up in multiplicity, that is, in forms and disintegration.

Placed on the fourth line, the Dragon prepares to quit the world, that is, to disappear, because having manifested, if it remained so, it would become intelligible to man and no longer be Perfection in itself. But it does not fly any further. "It is like the fish that jumps out of the water, with the will but without the means of disappearing: it is the *leaping Dragon*, equally ready to vanish in the ether of the celestial spaces and in the depths of the abysses, where is found the place of its repose." (*Yiking*, ch. 1, sec. 14; commentary by Tsouhi.)

The incessant activity, at the height of the leap, may take the Dragon's wings and disappear above, or keep the fish's fins and disappear below—hence, there is freedom to advance or to fall back. This is the symbol of the *liberty and independence with which the universe moves* and enters into its way (Tao). The situation is undetermined; but whatever the solution, we see that the true end of the movement of activity is absolute repose, which is beyond human power. (This is Nirvana, intelligible but inaccessible to the human being as we know it.)

Placed on the fifth line, the Dragon is fully manifested, acting in its plenitude and ruling the world. It has quitted the earth in order to vanish, but on the point of arrival at the limits, it has not yet disappeared, and its benevolent influence spreads everywhere: it is the *flying Dragon*, which in this instant obtains by its vision alone the golden age of humanity. It is the *happy expansion of the Universe in the Totality that has not ceased to be Unity*. The extreme activity makes this totality; the presence of the Dragon makes this unity. To put it in less metaphysical language, creation exists in its entirety, but it has no *forms*.

Let us recall that the fifth line is the median line of the upper trigram, and that it corresponds sympathetically to the second line. Note, too, that the second line is a will to action that is *not formulated*, and the fifth line is this non-*formal* action.

Placed on the sixth line, the Dragon disappears. "The proper height," says Tsouhi, "has been passed, the extreme unity is achieved, there is excess of elevation." Of course, this commentary should only be understood in relation to the visible universe. There it is the *"gliding Dragon,"* which begins to disappear—and along with it, that state of absolute perfection, which brought with it this regret for the impossibility of its lasting (because of both the relative perfection and the extreme activity of heaven). "That which is completely achieved," says Confucius, "cannot last long." And thus man is so imperfect that the very idea of perfection brings with it the fear of losing it. Here is the tangible creation, or rather *the divisibility of unity by the multiplication of forms*, and the establishment of duality relative to passive perfection. It is intelligible to man due to the disappearance of the Dragon, which symbolized Unity through the universal vehicle. It is the current state that we are passing through, in the cycle to which our humanity belongs. And the regret of this humanity engenders its unique desire that the psychologists may call the need for idealism, and which is basically the desire to re-enter the state of unity, to replace passive perfection by the activity that we can in no way understand, but which we know necessarily to exist. In short, it is the longing to *see the Dragon again.**

Such is the metaphysical harmony written on the part formed by the *Yiking's* first hexagram. It would take a whole book to deduce from it, even on this plane, all the elements of the relevant disciplines: Genesis, Creation, Cosmogony, Theogony, Theology, Ontology, Universal Synthesis, Origin of human Laws, and so forth. We are wary of entering into those tedious realms and their commentaries. Once the basis of knowledge is given, such a task is relatively easy, but it must be left as an interesting exercise (and also a commendable gymnastics)

---

*It is still understood that the symbolism of the Dragon, as explained here, is outside time and space, above individuals, and applicable only to syntheses. The next chapter will treat the symbolism of their progress in relation to what the West calls the creation of the visible Universe.

to the intellectual ability of researchers, whose mentality will thereby become better fit to comprehend the whole subject, and more adept at following the ensuing developments in their synthetic method.

But as we said at the outset, it is not only the metaphysical chord that has been struck on the staff of the hexagram of perfection. There are all the sciences beside metaphysics and its younger sisters; there are politics, social economy, ethics, divination. Each one finds through analogous working along this staff, and following the "*progress of the six Dragons*," solutions to satisfy all the intellectual needs of our humanity.

For example, let us see in a few lines how the initiate finds rules here for his conduct as magus, for his special practice.

Hidden Dragon—The gifted man should regulate his conduct according to the activity of Heaven. While he is not yet instructed, the will of heaven is hidden from his inadequate vision. He remains wrapped in his imperfect mortal coating. The gifted man should therefore meditate, be silent, and try to develop in study and contemplation. If he acted while the dragon is hidden, he would not show his true worth and would fall into an error prejudicial to his future.

Dragon in the Paddy Field—The gifted man is conscious of his virtue but cannot yet leave the earth.* Through his teachings, he gradually improves other beings, but he is not yet entitled to command them or to manifest himself. He should only set out to follow the fortune and example of the Magi who preceded him.

Visible Dragon—The gifted man, placed in a situation inferior to his merits, runs a danger. He must act with circumspection, for his virtue attracts the sympathy of the universe, and for this very reason the enmity of his superiors. But whether he retires

---

*One can grant this proposition all the psychic value that one wishes.

or remains, he must always take care to follow the normal way (*tao*).

Leaping Dragon—When the gifted man acts, it is never unconnected with the moment of action. He has increased his merits and his virtue in order to be noticed at a precise and definite moment. He is free to advance or retreat; he has preserved all his liberty; he can edify through his brilliant virtue, just as he can retire into commendable humility. In this situation, he should be guided by circumstances.

Flying Dragon—The gifted man occupies the superior situation that suits him. Arrived at the high peak of intelligence, he is pleased to see beneath him the man equally gifted with virtue, to aid him by his example and associate him to his power. When one is in full command of one's means, one should act.

Gliding Dragon—Infinite Beauty is hard to sustain. Thus, the gifted man should know when to advance or retreat, so as never to risk losing it. He must never commit excess in his actions, even good ones.

Likewise in the political sphere, the Dragons' progress defines the way of the Prince and the way of his subject. We will reserve its explanation for later. And to end an exposition that could go on indefinitely, we will just give the six simple and pregnant aphorisms of Confucius. With his usual clarity and concision, he adapts the Dragon's progress to the normal conduct of the simple citizen. This quotation will give a perfect idea of the way in which the Chinese sages understand the moral law.

1. Do not change fashion with the times; do not be eager for fame; flee the world; do not be upset by not being appreciated or known by others.
2. Good faith in the slightest words; circumspection in acts; be

on guard against lies; without bragging, improve your times by your transforming virtue.

3. Occupy a high situation without pride; occupy a lowly situation without complaining.

4. Perfect your talents; take advantage of the opportune moment.

5. Act and, by your actions, save the universe.

6. Avoid being too noble to have an occupation and being too haughty to have friends.

5

The Forms of the Universe

I am aware that in this extremely general presentation, the "Symbols of the Word" may have seemed even more vague than abstract. Their brilliance only appears if we arouse them by consulting the general text in view of a particular and precise adaptation.* We can now proceed to shed light on the Khien and the symbolism of the Dragons' progress by studying the tetragrammatic formula that Fohi's son-in-law, Prince Wenwang, placed at the head of the *Yiking* under that very ideogram.†

Wenwang's tetragram give a very concise key to the universal phenomenon commonly known as the "creation of the world." For the races that use the latter phrase, stating the fact of creation (commonly imagined as emergence from nothing) unconsciously begs the question and prepares innumerable metaphysical and logical difficulties. To have invented this word "creation" before having proved that it corresponds to an intellectual concept or a material event is a typical symptom of the state of the Aryan mind, deformed by the Semitic stamp. (And Jehovah alone knows how strong that stamp was!)

---

*One should remember this phrase, intentionally worded thus. It is the start of the whole divinatory science of the *Yiking*, naturally understood from the magical point of view, not from that "horoscopic" point of view which Far Eastern practitioners, like their Western brethren, know how to exploit.

†[Matgioi does not use "tetragram" in the same sense as "trigram" and "hexagram," which denote stacks of three and six lines. He uses it to refer to the four Chinese characters (*Uyan* [*Yuan*], *Heng, Li,* and *Tsheng* [*Zhen*]) that stand at the head of the *Yijing. —Trans.*]

Let us prepare ourselves right away not to sacrifice our logic to this incredible and very debatable *apriorism*. Wenwang's tetragram, whose generality alone saves it from abstraction, does not deny the fact of creation in itself, any more than it affirms it. The material realization or nonrealization of the idea does not seem at all important to the tradition. The tetragram situates the event outside time and space, thereby removing all objectivity from it, and keeping it in the domain from which we Westerners have no right to remove it: the domain of the pure idea and of metaphysical logic.

Perhaps all cosmologies, even the Sinaitic, could be summarized in a single doctrine, if we did not insist on dragging up to the level of universal creation the anthropomorphism with which we have sullied the divine plan—and if, under the pretext of homage to a creator whom we make into a man, we did not install the most concrete materialism in the heart of our peculiar modern religions.

We should, then, try to forget the conventional mediocrity in which the Western nations were cradled. And if henceforth we follow that advice, it seems certain that by applying it we will reap the greatest advantage from the Dragons' ascent through the Graphics of God.

But above all, we will be prepared to grasp Wenwang's tetragram in all its metaphysical abstraction, as the initial cause, the modification, and the final transformation of the Universe.

The tetragram, as an arcanum of the Universe, presents an alternative "staff," perhaps no less important from the point of view of the unification of the Eastern philosophic systems. In truth, all Taoism issues from Wenwang's tetragram, the very pith and marrow of the *Yiking*. When we come to study this admirable system of logic and pure morality, we will return to this filiation. For now, it is enough to state that by formulating these tetragrams, Wenwang was the precursor of Laotseu. The whole Taoist cosmogony is contained therein, and everything that will follow is pure Taoism.

We have already seen three times this mysterious hierogram of the Tao, which has so long remained incomprehensible. Without going into the observations that belong to another part of this work, we can say immediately that by *Tao* (which is usually and quite exactly translated as the *Way*) we understand the series, the sum, and the result of all the modifications of the Universe, or if one prefers, of the different states of Khien as manifested, independently of all objective relations.

UYAN: HENG: LI: TSHENG—*Initial Cause: Liberty: the Good: Perfection.* Such is Wenwang's IDIOGRAMMATIC TETRAGRAM. The *Yiking* adds these simple words, which are the "traditional commentary" on the formula:

How great it is, the initial cause of activity! All things owe to it the beginning of their constitutive ether; it is the whole heaven. The clouds pass by: the rain spreads its effects; the germs of beings perpetuate themselves in form. The universal life acts in an endless movement. The end and the beginning are illuminated by a great light. The way is modification and transformation: each thing conforms exactly to its nature and its destiny, and by attunement maintains the utmost Harmony; here are the Good and Perfection.

The traditional exposition of these arcana, which we will now explain, is the work of Wenwang's son Tscheoukong, collected and as it were codified by Tsheng-tse and Tsouhi. We have said that the objectively predominant quality of the Khien is activity—and activity radiates energy and will, thanks to which Being begins to show itself. The whole visible Universe is now in our evolutive circle and in the human state called "creation."

The determinative formula, as Wenwang states it in his four ideograms, manifests and "accompanies" the Universe from the germ of will that was its Genesis until its complete unfolding.

A. The voluntary cause (beginning) of all beings.

B. The possibility of creation (growth) of all beings.

C. The faculty of satisfaction (action) of the conditions of all beings.

D. The normal and perfect development (evolution) of all beings.

These four ideograms, which in themselves open and close the cycles of the Universe, are as popular as the crescent is to the Turks or the cross to the Christians. They have the advantage over humanity's other symbols of containing in explicit fashion the résumé of the entire doctrine as it applies to current humanity.

They have their *plane sigillary* expression in the graphic symbol of the Yin-yang (Taiky or Great-Extreme), which we will explain in the chapter treating the human condition.

The four states indicated by the formula of Wenwang's tetragram are called *qualities of substance* (Khien), but qualities altogether inherent, and integrating to the entity of *substance*. This is precisely how they differ from the sense that the West gives to the word *quality*, which however we cannot replace by any other. But we will have no trouble, because following the excellent Chinese method, this integrating quality is taken as the *substance* itself and identified with it, at least momentarily, for ease of comprehension: an identification that is also absolutely correct.

We will not give a new terminology to the cosmogonic system that we are studying here.

There is no need to try to familiarize the reader with the pronunciation of the ideograms. Imprecise as they are, we will continue with their translation into ordinary language: Initial Cause, Liberty, the Good, and Perfection.*

According to Tsouhi, the *Initial Cause of Perfection* (Khien-uyan) is the Great Principle from which the virtue of heaven results. It is above

---

*Whenever these expressions indicate one of the tetragram's parts, they will be printed in *italics*.

all the omnipotence of this principle that is considered, potentially including both Will and Force. Since the principle is active, the possibility of the birth of all beings constitutes its power and grandeur—and it is this grandeur that forms the beginning. The beginning of Being is the point of departure of its object, namely, the Principle of Causality, first manifestation of Perfection, genesis of all and especially of the three following terms of the tetragram. Moreover, it is the Principle of Causality considered in its efficient grandeur, namely the *Universal Cause*. After that, *Liberty* is only its free expansion; the *Good* and *Perfection* are simply its just consequence. It is simultaneously the purity of substance, the universality of cause, and the infinity of effect. Such is the metaphysical doctrine. From the cosmogonic point of view, it is the *position* or statement of the possibility of the Universe.

Here as elsewhere, one can see that there are volumes of deductions and considerations to be written. We have neither the leisure nor the space, and least of all the liking for them. We repeat that it is in the reader's mind that these deductions and reflections belong. We insist that he be no ordinary reader, but a studious and attentive one. As the tradition says, for his personal education he must be his own master and the collaborator of his guides. The work that we intentionally leave him to do is a sure guarantee of this indispensable collaboration, and of the fruitful excellence of his attitude.

Thus, the *Initial Cause* is the first attribute of Perfection (Khien), and there is identity between Perfection and *Initial Cause*. All the universes potentially emerge from the *Initial Cause*, where they are contained in germ. If one tries to set these two principles against one another, one will deduce the metaphysical impossibility of the existence of evil in itself. We will see multiplications, divisibilities, and divisions, from which come insufficiencies, objective obscurations, relative absences, but nowhere will we see evil *as a principle*. And everywhere, as proof of our metaphysical postulate, we will recognize that it has no existence. Along with this shameful dualism, this fatal error, this first misunderstanding, there vanish all the systems invented to abolish it, and all the heavenly repressions imagined to punish it.

There is no paradox here. We believe that we see evil in things we suffer from: it is a proof of our egotism and also a mark of our insufficiency. Evil only exists through the idea that we make of it for ourselves, by the belief we give to it: it only exists in us. And we see relative evil where we cannot see a link in the sequence of universal Good. The whole error comes from our insufficiency and our incapacity. This insufficiency comes from our relativity, namely, from our form; that is, from our analytic division; that is, from the multiplicity of beings. We will see that this multiplicity flows continually; that it is in time, that it is objective. Consequently, all concepts that are created within it and on its plane are not pure Ideas, nor aspects of Truth.

They are fugitive, unstable, erroneous. And among them, the concept of evil is the typical concept of our inadequate state of consciousness. To define metaphysically a mental state, dangerous only because it is so widespread, we should say that our concept of the existence of evil is created solely by this intellectual nonsense and this basic error, through which we unconsciously attribute to the objective and to relativities the character and function of the subjective and the absolute.*

Applied to existing humanity, the *initial cause* whose metaphysical expression we have just developed is nothing but the *Idea of Life*, the principle in virtue of which beings are engendered. Tsouhi says: "The idea of life is precisely humanity (Gen) in the sense of "*Solidarity of the*

---

*We will speak on this subject later in the study of Confucianism [a third volume to be entitled *La Voie Sociale*, which Matgioi apparently never wrote — *Trans.*], but we will repeat here a crude, even mediocre, yet very striking comparison. Light exists—*we see it*; darkness has no existence. There can be more light or less; there are no degrees of darkness. Even in the deepest of nights, there is a term to compare them with less deep nights. This term of comparison is precisely *light*, which subsists, diffused, even in the worst opacity. But absolute darkness does not exist; it is not even conceivable, because it could only exist if we could not see it; then it would escape the only sense that could know it—and that, in the objective domain, is nonsense.

species." This word *gen*, which, like "perpetuity," implies the community of existing beings, is the word most frequently repeated, even in ordinary conversation.

All who have traveled in China are astonished to notice the prominent place of this notion in the minds of all Chinese: a notion that is impersonal, refined, and *contrary to individualism.** But one should not think of it as a simple observance of traditional memory, without practical application.

The Far Easterner, with his habit of strict application, has drawn from this notion the immediate and highest consequence: that of *human solidarity* of which the *gen* has become the direct expression, and whose fraternal precepts are always and everywhere applied, as the first and also the most natural duty.

Thus, a metaphysical dogma comes down to the psychological plane and is put into practice on the social plane, so consistently as to become a habit and a need. From that derives the relative prosperity and the fruitful stability of the people and institutions. It would be interesting to test this statement against the social questions that so disrupt the West today, and by applying it down to its last corollaries, to show an original resolution of the utmost simplicity and perfection.

Here is how Tradition speaks on this subject: "If one imagines the sufferings of others in the light of the Idea of life, pity immediately arises; in the case of the revulsion that vice inspires, duty arises; in that of modesty, it is wellbeing and obedience to the Rites; in a matter of for and against, it is Reason."†

Thus stated, these alternatives explain the wonderfully logical consequences that are naturally deduced from them. We will study them when we tackle Confucian philosophy, but first we show that

---

*See remarkable examples in *La Cité Chinoise* by M. G. E. Simon, French consul in China (*Nouvelle Revue*, 1885).

†Tsouhi, *Sujets de dissertations*. [Article not known. —*Trans.*]

the general conduct of the people and the citizens is deduced in the following way: after recognizing what is needed for the existence and cohabitation of beings and the connections of their interests, one applies the same principle. In each particular case it transmutes itself into special qualities, all having as their essential basis the virtue of the tetragram. Thus, the wise man decides his actions by evaluating material and social objectivities through scientific and metaphysical subjectivity. It is upon the *Gen* (or the social Khien uyan), applied to the states of human life, that depend the birth and exercise of the qualities that render man good, which is to say, happy.

While the first term of the tetragram indicates the "Origin or gift of being," the second term (heng) expresses the "Liberty of Action of heaven." Beings, says the Great Commentary, now begin to enter the current of form. There is no distinction between them, but they are going to take hold: first, of *uniform* existence; then, of the exterior forms that distinguish them in our eyes. There is thus a *uniform* existence, then *multiform* existences. As for *informal* existence, it is not mentioned here, because it belongs precisely to perfection, and can only be mentioned therein. It is Eternity. Existence in itself does not, and logically cannot, partake of any species of creation; one cannot imagine a "spontaneous generation" on the metaphysical plane (nor perhaps on any other plane) without falling into absurdity. The "root" of the Universe is eternal and therefore ineluctable; all that exists, exists outside forms. Here that often obscured and misunderstood truth shines forth as an axiom: that all which is immortal is eternal.

If it were not to use an inappropriate term to express the false image of a correct idea, one could say that this "*Liberty*" represents the instant of the creative will just before the instant of effective creation. Between the first and the third term of the tetragram, the second is humanly impalpable, but necessary for the logic of the concepts.

A homely comparison will better bring out the value of the symbol. The water of a canal, held in on three sides by stone walls and on the fourth by the gates of a lock, is stable and immobile. When the lock suddenly opens, the equilibrium of the water changes and it falls abruptly into the lower reach. Let us suppose that the lock-gate is opened in a mathematical instant. This is not the instant when the water will start flowing but precedes it by the shortest possible interval; for the water only falls because the obstacle is removed, and the effect can never coincide precisely with its cause. There is, then, an imperceptible and fugitive moment when the water is no longer in equilibrium yet does not fall: it is only *going* to fall. This is the moment that in the tetragram of the Formation of the Universe constitutes *Liberty* (heng) between the potentiality of the creative will and the appearance of forms.

But on the metaphysical plane, this moment, which is both a geometric locus and a "state of universal consciousness," is unlimited. It if seems short to us, to the point of being ungraspable, that is only because the force that fills it is unintelligible to us, and because at this level our feeble senses confuse the notions of being and time, disengaged from the imperfections of action.

The third (li) and fourth (tsheng) terms of the tetragram, *the Good, Perfection*, immediately seem connected. The third term expresses the modification that form brings to beings; the fourth expresses the advantage that should result from that modification, if those who have received it each conform to their way: "The way of authority," says Tsouhi, "is progressive modification and transformation; transformation is the perfect accomplishment (or the end) of modification."

Before the third term, creation in the volitive state was identified with Being (creative will, active Perfection, Khien), and had not issued from it. After the third term it is still Being (Khien), but has flowed into the current of forms and consequently into the different beings as we know them. The advantage that results from the appearance of forms, following the will of heaven, gives the fourth term.

Tsouhi says: "The work of creation is the reason for life." Life is not in fact an inevitable corollary, but only one variety, an accident of creation.* The act of creation, at least essentially, does not entail the giving of life; for because of active Perfection (Being in itself) there is no place for an analogous and parallel existence. *To give life* is a crude translation of *to create form.* One of the forms into which Being and beings flow may be life, as we earthlings understand it. But it is only one of the innumerable forms of creation (modifications). Thus, creation does not include only all living beings: it also includes all nonliving beings, in other words, all forms. And let us note in passing that consciousness is by no means inherent in life.

Form is the direct means of modification; transformation is its definitive end, namely, the reintegration beyond forms (unity). It is through following this path and attaining its summit that the will of heaven is accomplished, and the fourth term of the tetragram is realized.

The sage Shipingwen has expressed in precise fashion (very rare in the Far East) the entire work comprised by the tetragram: "Modification is the mechanism that produces all beings; transformation is the mechanism in which all beings are absorbed." There is the whole Oriental genesis. There is no creation in the mechanical and material sense habitually attached to this expression, but there is production of Beings through modification of Being, and nothing more. One modification constitutes the present moment, of which we see an infinitesimal fragment in terrestrial life. Transformation indicates the return of beings in modification into unmodified Being and is the mechanism that presides over this reabsorption. The way of heaven thus includes both the emission into forms and the return out of forms.

From the human point of view, death is thus one of the moments of creation, without one being able to say whether it is the vestibule of

---

*Compare the Western intuitives: "The fever called 'Living' is conquered at last" (E. A. Poe).

transformation, or merely a modification that, in the normal course of activity, immediately follows the modification of life.

From the point of view of the "course" following the will of heaven, Shipingwen's text establishes the principle of involution and evolution, not perhaps in the sense of a descent and reascent, nor even explicitly in the sense of disintegration and reintegration, but in the sense of "voyage outside and return inside" via the current of forms, whose source and mouth merge (but whose mathematical image is *not* a circumference).

Now, modification and transformation comprise all the material or immaterial phenomena of creation since the emission of the will of heaven (*initial cause*). The first modification is the beginning of phenomena; the accomplishment of transformation, by the ending of the last modification, is the goal, the end of creation. All that is included in the third term of the tetragram: and the normal course of modifications and transformations (third term), conforming to the initial cause and following *Freedom*, produces *perfection* (fourth term) foreseen in the work of heaven.

The fourth term is thus the immediate and, as it were, imminent emanation of the unhindered third term. This means that on the human plane, man has only to develop according to his way for happiness to ensue. This is why the two last terms of the formula are said to be intimately bound to one another and should be studied together.

The consequence of Shipingwen's words is visible and intentional: it is also explicit in the texts of other commentators. After the perfect accomplishment of transformation, with the modifications absorbed, there is return to the beginning of the formula, namely, before the initial cause. Now, since all beings return to active Perfection (khien), and since that is essentially the Activity of heaven, the *Way* which has made them traverse the terms of the formula always exists and will exist eternally. Thus, there is departure in a new cycle that modifies and transforms itself as we have seen for any randomly chosen cycle—but nowhere is it said that the same beings have to flow into the same part of the current of forms. Translated to the human plane, this truth means that the forms subsist, modified and transformed by the same mechanism, but that formal beings cannot count on their past or present forms to presage their future forms. Creation does not change, but the formal parts, which reveal it to us, are the object of exchanges, or, if one prefers, progressions. The *essence* remains one, under diverse appearances, in the eternal succession of cycles, as it was one before the initial cause opened to the forms of the Universe the portals of the *Way*.

Let us phrase the formula mathematically and say that one conceives of transformation as a last cycle, which the four terms of the tetragram would exceed, without absolutely departing from the bosom of Perfection. Thus, we touch on the total truth about the final destinies of the Universe and of Humanity, the supreme and triumphant application of the Primordial Tradition.

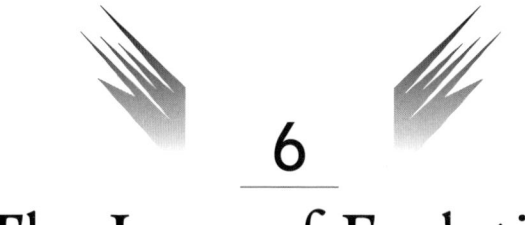

6

The Laws of Evolution

Some considerations in the preceding pages may have already helped one to foresee how this problem of the destinies of the Universe should be resolved, including the destiny of our present humanity (i.e., of everything in the current modification that goes by the name of humanity). It is not among the greatest problems, but from our personal point of view it is the most interesting.

The metaphysical activity of Perfection (Khien) extends to everything, and our destinies follow from it as a direct consequence. Our fate is regulated by the *universal Way* just as strictly as the forms of the Universe or any other concepts or entities, hence by the symbolic rise of the Dragons, from whose application nothing escapes.

But let us consider in general terms how to understand the destinies of the Universe, and how the concern for our earthly existence, for what precedes and what immediately follows it, is only a petty concern, and such a specialized case that neither the idea nor the very term of this existence deserves to figure, nor will really figure in the generalized explanation.

There is only one detailed application that we will study separately, because we currently depend on the human state. It is a very small aspect of the problem, not deserving special developments, and which owes them here only to the satisfaction that we feel obliged to give to the natural curiosity of the human being about the immediate end of his current modification and his passage to the next one, beyond and above this human state.

Let us emphasize here what has only been rapidly sketched above: The act of creation does not expressly or ineluctably involve the act of giving life, either of the earthly kind or something analogous to it. To "give life" is only one of the translations of "to flow into the current of forms." One of the forms into which beings flow may well be life, as we earthlings understand it; but it is only one of innumerable faces of our modifications. Life is therefore not an indispensable corollary, but only an *accident* of creation.

One must therefore take care, in all that follows, to ignore the impressions and the feelings relevant to our present state of consciousness and apply the reasonings to the succession of forms in general existence, not to particular existence in a single form. Only thus will one really comprehend the value of the system of the Chinese Magi and grasp their solution in all its synthesizing breadth.

As we have seen, Perfection is active; its activity is endless, free (i.e., consequent on its Principle of Causality), and good (i.e., regular and harmonic). Thus, all destinies of the Universe—past, present, and future (since "destiny" here does not imply the notion of the future)—are composed of activity, perpetuity, cause, and harmony.

Humanity is one of the forms into which beings flow (activity) in differentiating themselves from Being, formally and not essentially. It is thus one of the aspects of *passive* Perfection, and one of the modifications through which the Universe tends toward transformation, namely, to the mechanism of integration. Thus, Perfection is the generator of Humanity (causality), just as the one matter, eternal and formless, is the generator of divisible, diverse, and temporary matter. These are objective modes of subjectivity.

In precise metaphysical terms, humanity, considered even before its birth and also after its earthly death, is one of the Forms of the Universe (and earthly humanity is one of the modifications of this form). Likewise and equally scrupulously as all other beings, and without the possibility of the slightest special treatment, this form issues from Perfection thanks to the Principle of the Efficient Cause, traverses all the modifications, and attains the transformation through which it reintegrates Perfection. No form escapes this general law, and that is the *Harmony*: the harmony of the Way, the Tao, of which we here find the first and perfect definition, and which we will consider in depth in the philosophical system of Laotseu.*

We will state this ineluctable doctrine in plain language: Humanity comes from the Infinite; Humanity reenters the Infinite. We should even add that it never leaves it, and that all the modifications are produced alongside the Infinite: not only the Law of Harmony but good sense demand it. For if one fragment of Humanity did not follow the other fragments of this form, in all its modifications and in the final and communal transformation of the whole Universe, that fragment could only exit from the Infinite, exist outside the Infinite, be situated beside the Infinite. Now, if one can sometimes exit numerically from the mathematical Infinite, one cannot exist essentially from the metaphysical Infinite, on pain of destroying the notion and the very idea of that Infinite. This proof from absurdity may not entirely satisfy clairvoyance, but it nonetheless remains invincible.

We are all like the points on the surface of a cylinder, which may seem to belong to a straight line or to a plane tangential to this surface, but which are nonetheless an integral part not only of the surface but of the volume of the cylinder, as functions of that volume.

All of us—both visible and invisible forms of the Universe— emanate from the Infinite. We cannot exit from it, we are always tied to it by our essence—and after the forms we will remain in this Infinite,

---

*One should note henceforth that Laotseu's doctrine issues directly from the *Yiking* and the Primordial Tradition.

of which we never cease to be molecules, ungraspable and infinitesimal but imperatively necessary.

This doctrine constrains us as an axiom, and no revelation can ever pretend to impose a contrary belief. No quibbling over the value of consequences can prevail against this truth, so radiant that its mere demonstration is, so to speak, impalpable.

Although I do not want to enter into discussion here, one point needs to be explained, not so much for the useless effort of convincing opponents forever resolved to remain so, but to address the hesitation of certain consciences. The doctrine that we have expounded is not a pantheistic doctrine. That is the objection that science, conscience, and Western religions raise with habitual simplemindedness against the sacred traditions of India. The adepts of that tradition doubtless have no trouble in defending themselves against this emotional and irrational attack. But in what concerns us, we will not let this accusation of a crude idealism delay us for an instant and will immediately foresee and disprove it.

We are not pantheists; we have no right to declare that we are Gods, any more than the lost arm of the Venus de Milo has the right to declare that it is the Venus de Milo. The Universe has only its Essence; matter has only its substratum; nature and quality are also there. Together with the substratum, they make up the aspects of the metaphysical triad, which is just as true as the existences of the earthly Trinity, or the hypostases of the heavenly Trinity. We will return to this in detail when we come to psychology. We know, for now, that the metaphysical triad is certainly not the same as the heavenly Trinity, still less the Divine Unity, and that to say one will return to the bosom of God is not to say that one *is* God, otherwise all Christians would be the grossest of pantheists. In the metaphysical triad, Essence alone prevails over Perfection; but nature and quality depend on the current of modifications; like those, they are temporary and mutable, and can in no way belong to the Infinite—and the beings of which they are conditions and contingent but objectively indispensable functions, cannot be confused with the Infinite.

Let us speak for a moment in Western language, for here it perfectly fits the Oriental dogma, and thereby becomes, so to speak, the universal language. What distinguishes us from God is not essence, because we are of divine essence (and Christianity itself avows and advocates this origin). It is nature and quality, second and third terms of the metaphysical triad. This nature and quality are precisely the prerogative of beings entered into the current of forms; these are the terms that, in the succession of modifications, define form. One may say that in our eyes they themselves are *form*. But what, after all, *is* form? Geometrically speaking (and also philosophically), form is contour: it is the *appearance of the Limit.*

The limit, like form, is what determines us, specializes us, *divides us.* This divisibility ad infinitum, which is the entrance into forms, is what separates us from God. *Between God and ourselves, there is the Limit*, that is, the very determinant of all creation. And between God and ourselves there is nothing other than the *Limit*, because if it were suppressed, all creation would disappear, and only Universal Unity would remain.

Let us consider this theorem in depth, for it contains the entire explanation of the Universe, if we will remind ourselves that *Limit* or Forms, or the *Current of Forms* (for we are all speaking the same language here) does not only contain lines or shapes, as children think, but also the functions of weight, volume, density, and all the notions and perceptions that constitute the superficial and apparent differentiations of the molecules of Matter.

We have deliberately used an inferior type of terminology here, but we have done so in order to give more force to the most essential of the truths intelligible to man.

This demonstration will immediately define us in the mind of those who want classifications, genera, and species everywhere, and who think that scientists must absolutely be classed by chapters and by means of formulae. We are no pantheists, and even less "naturists." Being equally distant from pure mystics, who have no evidence but in mystery, and from materialists, who have no evidence than what the five human senses tell them, we are *positive idealists*.

We know that our reasoning and understanding are imperfect. Even so, we recognize in the control that they exercise over the perceptions and sensations given us by our human form that we cannot accept, like the materialists, whatever the examination of our senses declares to be truths and evidences. We are even forced to declare that these contingent truths and evidences cannot really be true or evidential, for the very reason that they appear to be so to imperfect instruments and inadequate observations.

But we cannot trust *a priori* and entirely the affirmations of our reasoning, any more than the experiences of our senses. For the first effect of our reasoning is to demonstrate our limited and incompletely extended reason. And it is limited expressly because it acts on a being that is in modification, in the current of forms, that is, within the limit. We should not protest against what the materialists call the unintelligible and reject as such. There are no *unintelligible* things: only things that are *currently incomprehensible*. And from the moment that we know ourselves to be far from perfect, that we are at an undetermined but not superior grade of evolution, we know that we cannot be universally comprehensive. Our understanding is at the cyclical stage of the other parts of the human compound. Consequently, far from rejecting the incomprehensible, we should declare that at our present level an apparent incomprehensibility is philosophically necessary, and that the presence of this relative incomprehensibility is a criterion—and the best one—by which we can recognize that we are going toward the truth. That is how we are not materialists by any means, and how, on the contrary, we are essentially idealists.

But we do not have a naive faith in these abstruse notions. And we refuse to build any psychological system, any moral rule, any sentimental religion on these currently mysterious abstractions. This unknown fills us neither with hope nor discouragement: only with curiosity and zeal. We feel—or rather, we *know*—that there is nothing fearful in this unknown, because its mystery does not lie in itself, but only in our contingency. Consequently, it is a relative mystery, destined to be solved by us on the day when the organ (which today is our physical eye) shall be sublimized to rise to the height of its vision. Our whole spirit should aspire to "lessen the distances," to see the limit disappear. We do not bend the knee to the mystery; we raise our understanding up to it. On that day we will have become the mystery itself—and from now on we can only laugh at the terrors and threats that are decreed in its name. And despite all, we claim that this audacity is the best way of arriving to knowledge. Even in Christian doctrine (which they try to tell us is the doctrine of genuflection) *heaven only belongs to the violent.** To try to penetrate the mystery is the only way our intelligences have of honoring it. He does not respect his father who turns his back on him, for fear of his face and glance. Our rule is to build nothing on the mystery, but to embrace it in order to comprehend it, knowing that our efforts, though incapable of success in our present state, are counted for us through our successive modifications for the final transformation.

This is how we are not mystical in the least, but resolutely positive. And this method has nothing against our idealist doctrine. On the contrary, it makes us better established in our mind. We think of what occurs daily in the indefinite progress of science, from Volta's frog to the electric solar waves; likewise, the indefinite progress of Humanity—which will change its name, its nature and quality, and preserve only its essence through all its modifications—will raise it to

---

*[Matthew 11:12. —*Trans.*]

the level of all the unknowns, whose last modification is to become axioms.

Thus, the Universe passes, until the final transformation, through all the modifications that the current of forms traverses. Let us determine the laws of this current. They conform to the Principles of Activity, Harmony, and the Good, through which Perfection manifests in Wenwang's tetragrammatic formula. And we should apply these principles to the laws of the current of forms in order to define its bases and elements, with an exactitude that belongs more to mathematics than to philosophy.

Beings proceed; they evolve. Such is the corollary of the initial principle, causality, which is the unique manifestation of Perfection, that is, the *will of heaven.* Could one conceive of them stopping? No, for to cause such a stop would suppose a will of heaven contrary to that which keeps them in motion, and it is abnormally impossible for heaven to manifest two principles contrary to one another. Thus, from the moment that movement comes into being (and that is something one cannot deny, even objectively), there will always be movement, and it can be defined as the *Eternal Manifestation of Perfection.* Thus, the Principle of Causality is satisfied. But to avoid any possible error in our minds, even for an instant, we add that one must not confuse the Eternal Movement with an "eternal creation" or an "eternal passage in the current of forms." We will define elsewhere what Eternal Movement and Eternal Act are, but it would be childish presumption to pretend to give a *direction* to the *Totality* of movement, or a *motive* to the *Totality* of actions. Thus, even before the definition, one can comprehend the final end to which the Principle of Causality leads.

How does the Law of Activity cause beings to evolve? The continuity of evolution only satisfies causality; *activity* requires an *action*; an action of any kind satisfies activity—but does the repetition of any action really constitute an action? We have to reply no, for from the point of view of action itself, its repetition constitutes *monotony*—and from the point of view of the motors of action, we see that the same action is engendered by the same motors, acting under the same impulsion, with the same force. The *continuity* of an action is therefore not activity; it is, on the contrary, after the movement has started, the *immobility* of the motoric principle. Consequently, the Principle of Activity is not satisfied by a single action, nor by the same action repeated twice or more, but only by an indefinite series of actions, which are due to different motors, and which consequently cannot be absolutely identical. Hence, in the name of the Principle of Activity, *one does not pass twice through the same current of forms.* And it absolutely forbids us to believe in metempsychosis, at least the brutal and crude metempsychosis that has been extracted with great pains from Buddhist and Pythagorean doctrines, and which is not really found there.*

But on the contrary, after having exhausted one form and all the circumstances of a modification, we pass invincibly to another modification, with the logical certitude that we will never return to what we have just left.

How can *continuous* and *varied* movement accord with the Law of Harmony, which is the third term of Wenwang's tetragrammatic formula? (We note in passing that the Law of Harmony can only be satisfied by varied actions, for there is no harmony in repetition: harmonic relations, like algebraic and geometrical ones, can only be established between different quantities.) Harmony is satisfied by the proportions (in the mathematical sense) of the variations; that is, any form is invariably distant from the preceding and following ones, and all modifications are invariably distant from each other. Thus, the series of modifications can be translated mathematically by an arithmetic or geometric progression, tending toward a "metaphysical place" that one cannot objectively think of attaining. Thus, the Law of Harmony truly manifests.

---

*The Law of Rebirths is something entirely different. But we must assert straightaway that it is real and logical, with all the fortunate consequences that humanity expects from it, both from the point of view of its end and from the point of view of its personality.

This has another consequence that immediately concerns beings in modification: it is the invariability of direction and sequence of modifications through which all beings pass. For just as activity prohibits passing twice through the same form, harmony decrees that one cannot fail to pass through all the forms, hence that there are many currents of forms. In this logical necessity, we humans henceforth find a pledge of the fraternity of our spirits and the parallelism of our efforts.* As for those who unite their tendencies in the course of one modification, their union is by the same token indestructible, whether or not they preserve its memory; they will find themselves analogically side by side in the modifications to come.

Finally, the fourth law means that *continuous, varied,* and *harmonious* movement is beneficent and leads the Universe to Perfection. Here the inflexible logic of the Chinese Magi brings us the clearest vision of our destinies. Willed by Perfection, determined by the precise consequences of that will, Evolution cannot be otherwise than good, and can only produce an excellent result for the beings who are its material. Remember that there is no reintegration outside Perfection. There is no place—physical, geometric, or metaphysical—outside Perfection. There is thus nothing else than the happy final reintegration. Such is the necessity of the fourth law. But if we combine its effects with those of the third law, we realize immediately that there is no essential difference in the destiny of beings in modification: there is no place for "falls" of any kind, which would contravene the Law of the Good, if the falls were general, and the Law of Harmony, if they were partial and temporary. The passage of beings through the modifications of the Universe is thus a regular ascent—continuous, harmonious, and beneficent—in which Perfection, of which we are infinitesimal fragments and continuous emanations, could not do otherwise than include us.

---

*We will return to this at length in "Conditions of the Individual" (ch. 8).

Here, very briefly explained (for the Chinese have written volumes about it, and Western philosophers would not fail to do likewise) are the generators of Universal Evolution. They are so characteristic, so ineluctable, so precise that no honest human intellect can possibly reject them. Moreover, following the best of methods, we can reduce the Destinies of the Universe to a geometric design as easily as we reduced to six lines, without demeaning it, what the West calls the "incommunicable Eternal."*

The Principle of Causality manifests through movement. In mechanics, all movement is represented essentially by a line. Since the Principle of Activity manifests through indefinite diversity, this line cannot be a circumference, nor a broken line: it can only be a line with hyperbolic or parabolic elements, such as comets seem to describe in space, and whose branches extend to infinity. This hypothesis of course supposes that we are only considering a single plane of space: but the Principle of Harmony here satisfies the *cyclical* idea and symbolizes at every point the idea of *return* and the Principle of Reintegration. Thus, the Principle of Harmony requires that modifications should occur at equal intervals and equal distances from each other. This eliminates any possibility of a plane line, because there are *relations of distance* between its different parts. Therefore, the line of universal movement is inscribed on a *curved surface*, and the distances between the elements of this line are in arithmetical progression, to satisfy the Law of Harmony. Finally, the Law of the Good demands that the modifications continually ascend, so that the elements of the figure are inevitably and invariably *superimposed* on one another.

The graphic requirements can be summarized thusly: a line (Principle of Causality): indefinite and never passing again through the same points (Principle of Activity): definition of curves, intersections of curved surfaces, winding above each other (Principle of the

---

*It will be easy for us, later on, to demonstrate how the free will of the *human species* fits very well into the general laws established above.

Good): and that all the points of an element should be equally distant from the corresponding points of the higher and the lower element (Principle of Harmony).

The one and only surface that would satisfy these conditions is the cylindrical helicoid. In this, the line of universal movement will be precisely the intersection of the helix (curved surface) with the lateral surface of the cylinder representing cyclical Evolution, along which all beings are moving. Of course, the cylinder of Evolution is only representative from the point of view of visualization, which obliges it to intersect the indefinite curved surface in order to obtain the helix. The surface along which the helix winds has no physical or geometric location: it can be extended at will to infinity, or imagined as reduced to the height of the cylinder alone. Likewise, the radius of the base of the cylinder is indifferent, and in reality is equal to zero in the metaphysics of numbers.

The only element of the helix that remains to be determined is its pitch, namely, the distance along the height of the cylinder between two corresponding points of its curve. (The curve contained between these two points makes one revolution of the helix, and all the revolutions are equal.) This pitch of the helix is constant (Principle of Harmony) and is the only datum that we can determine mathematically, because we are in the course of a revolution, and have lost the memory of our passage along the preceding revolutions.

Let us construct this very simple and entirely satisfactory figure. From any point on the helix, draw on the lateral surface of the cylinder a parallel to the height of the cylinder. That will determine a moment of Evolution, and one entire modification.

The Universe (all beings) is, by the Principle of Causality, set in motion and propelled along the helix inscribed on the face of the cylinder (the cylinder, we repeat, is hypothetical and represents the manifestation of the will of heaven, which includes all the movements issued from it, supposing it to have stopped for a moment).

Let us take it at the point mentioned above and suppose that this point is the start of one modification. At the moment when the Universe enters this modification, if it were left to itself, it would follow a trajectory represented precisely by the tangent to the helix at the given point. But it is breathed out by the will of heaven (Principle of Activity) and aimed toward heaven (Principle of the Good). Thus, it describes the helix as indicated, and the pitch of the helix is precisely the mathematical distance of the *"attractive force of the Divinity."* There is no direct method of appreciating this distance; one could only know it through analogy (Principle of Harmony), if the Universe, in its present modification, could remember its past modification, and thus estimate the metaphysical quantity that has been acquired, and consequently measure the ascending force. We are not saying that it would be impossible, for it is easily comprehensible, but it is not within the faculties of present humanity.*

During the whole course of the Universe along the revolution of the helix that represents its present modification, the elements controlling it are analogous (Law of Harmony) and nonidentical (Law of Activity) to those which controlled it in past modifications and will control it in future ones. The study of the present modification of the Universe can thus, if well undertaken, obtain by analogy precise information on the past and future destinies of all beings. This is a useful work for those who can devote themselves to it.

On arrival at the end of this particular revolution in the helix, the Universe reaches the end of its modification and passes into a following one which is superior, as required by the Principle of the Good. But the helix is regular throughout and in all its points; between the end of one modification and the beginning of the next, there is no break or sudden change. The passage from one modification to another

---

*We can see here that those who take the *circle* as the symbol of Evolution have simply forgotten the *first cause.*

happens as logically and simply as the passage from one situation to another within the same modification. The universe always moves normally and with an equal movement (Law of Harmony). The passage is *insensible*; there is nothing *surprising* or *painful* about it.

The Universe thus passes into the next modification, where it successively occupies analogous positions (Law of Harmony) on a higher curved surface (Law of the Good). And this movement lasts throughout Evolution. Will it be eternal—will modifications succeed one another for ever, and will the helix revolve endlessly around a baseless cylinder? Some have said so, supported by the principle that the will of heaven, having manifested movement, could not stop it. But it is very wrong to conceive the movement of the heavenly will as inherent in the passage from one place to another, that is, as a displacement, in whatever world one cares to imagine this displacement. We will see in the Book of Laotseu, explaining the *Yiking*, that the "celestial movement" agrees very well, on the metaphysical plane, with what we call *repose*. So, this is not a serious objection.

When will the series of modifications be exhausted? The Universe that traverses them will know, when it knows not only the measure of the helix's pitch, that is, the attractive force of the Divinity, but also the distance that, at the summit of the ideal cylinder, separates it from Perfection.

What does it matter that we cannot determine this at present, if we know how we will do so later, by the appreciation of elements and the acquisition of faculties that are lacking in the human state?

Once more, the logic of mathematics consoles us for our inadequate intelligence.

The figurative cylinder around which the evolutive helix winds following the Principle of Activity, rises to infinity. Now, since parallels meet at infinity, the lateral surface and the height of the cylinder meet at infinity in a single point, and the limit of the cylinder is a cone. This is the figure that mathematics presents when we consider the end of modifications, that is, the moment of Transformation, and the Idea of Reintegration. The mathematics here is absolute, and of striking precision. All the elements of the lateral surface of the volume and, consequently, the helix that develops there, converge toward a single point at the top of the cylinder (now the vertex of a cone). The hypothetical extremity of the cylinder's height is, as we have seen, the center of attraction of the will of heaven; thus, it is *exactly* at infinity that *the evolved Universe coincides with Perfection.* The Universe cannot go further, *even mathematically,* nor escape from Perfection by another current of forms. Reintegration in the bosom of Perfection is the total and inevitable destiny of all beings.

If one presses further the analogical symbol presented by the geometric figure, one may claim that after having been absorbed in Perfection, the Universe distinguishes itself anew. For a cone, even one generated by a cylinder imagined to infinity, involves another conical branch opposed to the first at its vertex. Thus, the Universe would depart along a new conical helix, the branches of the nappe* spreading to infinity. Nothing opposes this mathematical truth, but it cannot be transposed symbolically to metaphysics. For mathematical infinity assumes Riemannian surfaces and transfinite numbers—and more simply, at every moment of algebraic discussions, one is led to conceive of a notion beyond the infinite. This is the best demonstration that mathematical infinity is not metaphysically infinite, but indefinite. Heavenly Perfection is not situated in the indefinite, but in the Infinite. Even if we can take the indefinite as an image of the infinite, we cannot apply to the latter the reasonings of the former. Symbolism works downward, never upward.

Let us then greet with confidence the designs of the *will of heaven,* still unknown yet logical and intelligible, and fearlessly follow the course and end—which cannot be otherwise than happy—of the Destinies of the Universe.

---

*[Nappe (Fr. and Eng.) = one of two surfaces of a double cone partitioned by the vertex of the cone. —*Trans.*]

7

The Destinies of Humanity

If one takes the cylinder and the helix as representing the destinies of the Universe, regulated by the Laws of Evolution, one will notice that the special destinies of Humanity are regulated by the same laws, in an equally exact and indisputable fashion. All it needs is a logical and appropriate application of these laws, in order to have the solution to the problems that trouble our species to a greater or lesser degree.

The human cycle is one of the elements of the helix, probably one of its turns. Human life can then be defined as beginning and ending with the relevant turn, limited at both ends by the two intersections of the turn with the parallel to the cylinder's height, drawn through any point on its lateral surface.

This corollary of our preceding propositions immediately shows that the human cycle is an entirely normal cycle. The human modification, among all the others, has nothing surprising or marvelous about it, and there are no special solutions or transformations to be applied to it.

We must insist that there is nothing extraordinary about humanity, nor about the fate that awaits it. The only thing that would be extraordinary is if it were not as it is. In its natural place it shares in the modifications of the Universe; it is one of the normal elements of Evolution. Nothing has been *created* for man; nothing special awaits him. He has come from where everything emerges; he goes where it all returns—and the state in which he finds himself has no more importance than the others.

We grant humanity a greater importance because that is where we currently find ourselves, which is quite reasonable if we simply feel a stronger curiosity about it. But it is nothing but naive vanity if this curiosity leads us to claim a special treatment for man. We must be convinced (which is difficult for our pride and for those who seek advantages from it) that man is not in an inferior situation, nor in a privileged situation; he is simply as he should be. He is not a particularly happy being, nor particularly unhappy, and he does not deserve either the exaggerated compliments or the pitiable execrations with which religious texts alternately inflate or stupefy him.

"Only man has a soul," cry certain adulators who, like all of their kind, are trying to profit from their flattery. This proposition is as patently false as the claim that only man has a body. And, in reality, this proposition is as false in its general sense as in its pretension. Man certainly has something that is special to him, as we will explain later: it is the very characteristic of the human state. But the modified beings that follow and precede us possess just as much the posthuman and the prehuman characteristics, and have no right to boast of the fact since it is the Law of Activity that has granted them, and they could not fail to acquire them successively.

But what characterizes the human being, as with any other being, is not some unique element that is only found in man. It is a *compound* whose quantities are only found in man in certain coefficients, but whose consecutive elements are found in one or more adjacent states. They are not *of man*; only *their association* makes the human being.

The mathematical diagram shows us a perfectly regular and coordinated helix. No point is eccentric; all are regular and consequent on the generating elements of the figure. Humanity is on one of these points, or, better, on one of the turns composed by these points. It is therefore entirely normal, with no *preferences on the part of the Divinity*. We should relegate to the old arsenal of our prides and terrors the praises and threats that have been solemnly imparted in the name of this *privileged situation*, which is nothing but a foolish concept, entirely contrary to the Principle of Evolution and of Perfection itself.

Let us examine the helix of Evolution at a point of intersection made by the parallel to the cylinder's height on its lateral surface. This parallel cuts every revolution of the helix. The turn of Humanity is depicted between two consecutive points of intersection. The lower point of intersection is that of the beginning of the turn, and of our current observation. It is the moment at which Humanity is born.*

It is born, which is to say that it comes from the preceding modification, without clash or shock, rising with the gentle curve by a continuous gyratory movement due to the attractive force of Perfection. The Law of Causality is the *origin* of this birth and of the perpetuity of this birth, at least while there is a current of Forms: for the human form can be absorbed in the Universal. It will certainly be absorbed in it, but it cannot perish, in the negative sense that we give to that grammatical term. It will quietly finish when its form expires and is replaced by another, but it will not suddenly be terminated by a brutal cataclysm that would break the uniform course of its destiny. Without further and tedious discussion, let us leave the *end of the world* to Good King Robert,† and the congelation of our globe to Monsieur Camille Flammarion. These hypotheses are gratuitous, and even if one considers them as materially and physiologically realizable, they would have no influence on the human Form, nor on the Destinies of Humanity. The earthly globe, as a vehicle, could only perish when it had become unnecessary. That is to say that humanity would not perish along with the planet, but that the planet would perish when it no longer served as

---

*We say *Humanity* and not *man* in particular. We are here studying *collective man*. It is the free will of the species that makes *individuals* out of collective man.

†[King Robert the Pious, ruled France 996–1031, during and after the popular fear that the world would end in Anno Domini 1000. —*Trans.*]

a theater for Humanity. And all these are only superfluous and redundant contingencies.

The Law of Activity drives Humanity from its birth on the spiral of its particular evolution. Humanity never remains immobile on one point of this spiral and never passes twice through the same point. Does that mean to say that the human cycle consists solely of terrestrial life, and that after our death we must never return to the planet? It would be a fortunate person who could provide a definitive answer to this question, in either direction. Certainly, we will never pass again through the human state such as we are passing through it today, since the Law of Activity, the Law of Harmony, and the Law of the Good would all be contravened thereby. But are "human compounds" only found on earth? And is it only on earth that "human compounds" can be modified? We will try to respond by analogy to such uncomfortable questions.

In the three realms that we know on our globe, the animal realm sees and feels the vegetal and the mineral realm; the vegetal is aware but does not see; the mineral is neither aware nor sees.* This completes all that falls under the five senses. But we are aware, without seeing it, of a different kind of matter from what is catalogued in these three realms. Electricity, psychic energy, errant forces: these are forms of matter that do not fall under our sensory control. Our relation to them is like the plant's relation to humanity. We can press the analogy further. The mineral cannot feel us casting and making use of it. We could be the perfectly unconscious instruments of terrestrial beings who have none of our five senses, of whom we are unaware, and who are using our mind without our knowledge exactly as our will makes use of the mineral.† We govern the beasts, the plants, the metals: why, if it is not

---

*That, at least, is the state of current experimental science.
†Suggestion [hypnosis] gives humans the power over other humans who lose their will to the will of their temporary masters. It would thus be foolish to claim that our hypothesis does not rest on experimental data as well as on analogy.

through the most ridiculous pride, do we not want to be governed by anyone, and for there to be no form in the Universe between God and ourselves? That is totally illogical and even begins to be contrary to recent discoveries of the mental and psychic sciences. These superior beings, these unknown but undeniable entities, these absolutely normal forms of the Universe—are they or are they not sublimized Humanities? Who would dare to insist that they are? But who would dare to say that it is impossible?

On the other hand, is the human cycle inevitably limited to the role that we see it playing on this earth? Is it indispensable for man to remain in humanity that he should tread the ground with his feet, gather wheat with his hands, tear meat with his teeth? No one will claim that the essence of Humanity is in the *form*, or to use a more physical language, in the possession and use of the five senses and in the habitat of our current planet. Humanity can develop outside the planet, with an appearance and means appropriate to the formal conditions of existence that will be reserved for it elsewhere. This is perfectly analogical and plausible.

Thus, for Humanity, here are two equally acceptable variations of the Law of Rebirths: either to be on this earth with other organic elements, with another *Life*, or else to pass to another modification with analogous though perfected organs. Such is the Buddhist and Pythagorean metempsychosis, which all of antiquity admits, and which we too admit as a perfectly logical and proven corollary of the Laws of Evolution. This Law of Rebirths affects Humanity in the whole human cycle; one of its applications is in the earthly human species— and that is why we have been making a distinction between collective Man and individual man.

Humanity is one turn of the helix; the current human species is one of the points of the turn.* Let us beware of confusing them, of

---

*And it is that which can be symbolized by the *circle of life*, characterized by the Yin-yang, that we will study later.

taking the point for the whole, and let us not fall into nebulous reveries or crude transformism. Earthly human life is one of the points of the human cycle; it is one of the forms of Humanity—and Humanity, through the Law of Rebirths, traverses the present human state without staying there and without returning to it. But if the human species is lost to man after individual death, Humanity remains for the collective Man. And we will see later how the human aggregate behaves in these different situations. We will also see that both before and after the human cycle there subsists, from what makes the characteristic of Humanity, an immanent and eternal constitutive element.

The Law of Harmony drives Humanity along its cycle with a general and uniform motion. The motion is general, in that none of the fragments that make up Humanity can escape it by chance or voluntarily quit it. It is uniform in that the initial cause (the movement due to the manifestation of the will of heaven) is exerted on all of Humanity in an always equal manner, and that Humanity moves along its turn without a bump or halt. This Law of Harmony has a triple consequence: in Humanity's fate there is no chance; there is no essential differentiation; and there are no surprises or exceptions.

There is no chance. Chance is an effect produced by the concordance of the unconsciousness of the element with the absence of its initial motor. We willingly admit that an element may be unconscious, due to shortcoming in the course of a modification, and of want of intellection if one considers the series of modifications. But how could we admit the absence of the motor, namely the oblivion in which the Will of heaven would leave the least of the fragments that the Principle of Causality has thrown into movement, that is, into objective existence? That is altogether impossible, for if that fragmentary element were left to chance *outside* the manifested Universe, one would have to deny the infinitude of the Will of heaven; and if the element were left to chance *inside* the manifested Universe, one would have to deny the omniscient Perfection of that Will. That would be to say that this Will of heaven did not exist. *Chance* and *heaven* are contradictory and exclusive of one another. And since the Universe is heaven manifested, we must deny either chance or the Universe, against the most concrete evidence of our senses. Thus, we are brought to this true proposition: *Chance does not exist.* And we are happy to state that this proposition has long been inscribed on the threshold of purely Western high science, and at the head of the works of the masters who have concerned themselves with it. In Christianity—and in all the religious and philosophical works that emanate from it or from which it emanates—this efficient part of the Principle of Harmony bears the name of *Providence*, a word whose radical significance constitutes the very negation of chance.

There is no differentiation within Humanity between the destinies of the different elements that compose it. The elements that, at a given point, enter simultaneously and harmoniously into a modification, emerge together from this modification and enter together into another one. Moreover, all the elements traverse all the modifications in the same order. Finally, just like their origin, their end is the same for all. This is what the Law of Harmony strictly wills—and it is impossible for this law to be violated in any of its points. We will see in the sequel to these studies, when we take the texts of the Kan Ying, or Sanctions, how the crude doctrine of eternal Recompenses and Punishments is transformed, when those who teach it have no money or influence to gain from inspiring terrors in believers. We must assert henceforth that the equally inalterable Principle of Justice always and everywhere obtains perfect satisfaction. But it is a property of the attributes of heaven all to conform to each other, and not to obstruct one another even in their remotest consequences. The Principle of Justice fits perfectly well with the Law of Harmony, of which it is a metaphysical manifestation—and Harmony, like its corollary of Justice, wills that the final destiny of Humanity and of the Universe should be a common and unique destiny.

We remark in passing that the neither the application of Harmony nor the application of Activity allows us to admit the brutal metempsychosis of Pythagoras's inferior successors. Elements could not remain in a modification—whether keeping or changing their forms—while other elements, entered at the same time into this modification, traversed and departed from it. The former elements could not advance while the others retrograded under the pretext of sanctions; once and for all, the sanctions attached to temporary acts are necessarily objective and cannot apply to laws consequential on subjectivity. All beings follow a harmonic and regular movement in the current of forms, and it is the Law of the *Good* that alone determines the direction of this movement.

Finally, in this movement there is no bump, shock, or surprise—that is to say, its course is *methodical*. Harmony affects all beings in their passivity and regularizes their emission into forms. There is thus no unintentional creation, no *spontaneous generation*. All beings existed at the same time, and the first day that we are aware of their existence is not the day of their birth. This pretension is another result of the pride of human brains served by an imperfect intelligence and by sense organs that are really quite mediocre. It is no more sustainable than the opinion of some astronomer (who, for the honor of astronomy, I believe doesn't and never will exist) who declared that a star was created on the day when he first perceived it in his telescope, while really this star was so far from our globe that the light emitted from it had only just reached us. It would be ridiculous to refuse to the principles of metaphysics and the manifestations of subjectivity what one accords to the laws of a minor science. So, there is no spontaneous generation. But the regularity of emission of forms demands more: it wills the regular transmission of form, and it wills it down to the least detail. Thus, the human *form* will always be the human *form*. It is just as impossible for a man to engender a bull as for a bull to engender a man, or a plant to engender a piece of metal. Saying that may seem ridiculous but is much less so when one understands that it expresses the impossibility that an ape could engender a man, via any imaginable improvements or stages. And that irredeemably condemns the bizarre Littréan theory* that has been clumsily decorated with the name of Darwinism. The latest holders of these propositions, unprovable physically or metaphysically, will not admit for a moment that a Black couple can procreate a White, yet they find it plausible that a couple of orangutans, deep in the jungle and in an impenetrable mystery, should one day have spawned a human being!

We suppose, of course, that just as there is no appreciable limit between the most animal of vegetables and the most vegetal of animals, there are any number of forms between the human form and the other animal forms closest to it, and that when sorted and ranked they are as similar as possible to their neighbors. Between the most humanoid ape and the most simian human, there might be a thousand forms of anthropoids (although absolutely convincing traces have never been found either in geology or zoology). Thus, the distance between man and ape will be filled to the satisfaction of certain scholars, very proud of themselves and very modest about their ancestors. That is true as far as similarity of appearances goes, but the differentiation between the ranks, though indefinite or infinitesimal, is as strict as ever: anthropoids make anthropoids; monkeys make monkeys; and humans make humans. And so it will be as long as the current of forms flows in the Universe.

We now know this Humanity to be active, mobile, and, after its movements, destined to a general and common fate. The Law of the Good prescribes this fate for it, and at the same time the direction and end of its activity. This end is excellent, for the supreme and unique design of the will of heaven is essentially and invincibly good. There are no eternal terrors or sufferings, as we shall show in the briefest and most basic language.

If a state of suffering existed eternally outside God, then God

---

*[Reference to Émile Littré (1801–1881), materialist philosopher and lexicographer. —*Trans.*]

would not contain all; he would not be infinite; he would not be God. If suffering existed eternally within God, he would not be infinitely good; he would not be God. Thus, eternal suffering does not exist, either within God or outside him. That is to say, it does not exist at all and *cannot* exist. The most eloquent threats, the most self-interested vituperations do not escape this simple dilemma, to which the whole argument is confined.

Besides, it is expressly the will of heaven that emits beings in the current of forms. Without this Eternal Will, neither movement nor Form, nor the least part of the *"creation"* would exist. How could one suppose that this will, which is exercised at birth and during all the modifications of beings, would not be exercised at the moment of the final transformation? Would it let it wane or collapse? How could this will, exercised eternally, lead the beings issued from it, and from it alone, to an end of suffering and misery? How could one imagine it not guiding them? How could it guide them anywhere but to itself, namely, to an end identical with the beginning? These are pretentions without logic, without justice, without goodwill; they are utterly repellent and smack of their human origin, namely, a mediocre and particularist one. Only a narrow-minded entity could conceive of a solution contrary to the Good, in other words, a negative one. And by the fact that a solution is negative and limited, it cannot get out of the contingence in which it was engendered, and it is inapplicable to problems that come under the subjective category.

Here, then, are the destinies of Humanity, perfectly directed by the four inescapable laws that have presided over its birth and preside over the course of the Universe. But with that inescapability, what becomes of the freedom of things? We will explain it emphatically when we come to the conditions of the individual. Human freedom does exist, and it exists in conditions that satisfy subjective justice and sufficiently engage our personal responsibilities from the point of view of the expected consequences.

But that being said, and needing to be explained elsewhere, *the freedom of beings does not exist*, insofar as they are fragments thrown into the current by the will of heaven, and having to be retrieved by that will. Let us not forget to which world the series in question belongs, and that our reasoning applies on the metaphysical—that is to say, divine—plane. We are here face to face with the Divine Will. No will exists unless it emanates from this will; hence no will can equal it, for if a will equaled the Divine, it would *be* the Divine, and not its emanation.

Any will equal to the Divine is identical to it; thus, no will can set itself up *with equality* against the divine Will. Thus, no will triumphs over the Divine; *hence there is no liberty against the Activity of heaven.* The designs of heaven cannot be reversed, crossed, or retarded: nothing can prevail against them, and all religious doctrines—even that of Rome, expressed in the world's worst Latin (*et portae inferi non praevalebunt*, etc.)—accord here with metaphysics and natural logic. Total Freedom exists only in the Infinite, and only acts through the Infinite and within the will of the Infinite. A being flowing in the current of forms cannot be endowed with total freedom, without it immediately becoming God. The universe is invincibly ruled and moves invincibly toward its destinies. And just as man is not born when he wishes, and does not choose the moment of his death, Humanity is born into one modification and quits it under conditions foreseen by the will of heaven. And it arrives where the will of heaven has directed it, from all eternity.

Total Freedom is the most dangerous and most ridiculous gift ever offered to Humanity: dangerous, because it could oppose fortunate destinies; ridiculous, because those who pretend to grant it have not considered that in allowing Humanity to stand up to God, they are making Humanity into God. But this invention of pride and human cupidity cares little for such a contradiction joined to such impiety. *Total Freedom*, which the human species accepted out of pride, led to

Total Responsibility, to *Total Fault*, and to *Eternal Punishment*, the only possible reparation for this total fault. And the inventors of the theorem and its consequences had pretended at the same time that as ministers of God on earth, they could save one from *Eternal Punishment* through prayers, money, and advantages of every sort, thereby remitting the *Total Fault*, directing the *Total Responsibility*, and thus by an ingenious repercussion, pay for this *Total Freedom* of which they had made a free gift to benevolent Humanity.

We are well aware that we are destroying the liveliest prejudice of the species, by depriving it of a danger that it can hardly believe to be imaginary, along with its appointed protectors against this danger, and because, if we were heeded, we would deprive those protectors of the easy livelihood that they enjoyed, and the easy influence with which they reigned for centuries. We know that we are attacking a conviction deeply embedded in the conscience that our ancestors, our educators, and innumerable years have given us. We are just as keenly aware of the difficulty of this task. In our own case, after having irrevocably established our certitude, the leaven of ancient terrors sometimes still ferments and arouses the hereditary fear that plagued our infancy. It is difficult to free one's mind and reason from the most unacceptable shackles when they are age-old, and when they borrow the authority of those who taught us and those whom we have loved. But in all truth, it is impossible for us to admit, even once, the victory of irrational sentiment over logic, and to believe that God should have consented to be equal to man, precisely to make him miserable, and that the "*creator*" enjoyed declaring Himself unable to make his "*creature*" inevitably happy, in that "*eternity*" which He has given him and which the creature never asked Him for.*

Certainly, we are not denying any of it—for on the relative plane

---

*We are deliberately using the most blatant language here, so that what we want to say will be blazingly evident to all. [In this unique case, Matgioi capitalizes the pronouns referring to God. —*Trans.*]

and in the world of contingencies there are enough liberties to flatter pride, enough sanctions to content justice, enough "penitences" to satisfy lovers of the worst emotions (as we shall soon see). But that the will of heaven, from all eternity, should have regulated and prepared the modifications and the transformation of the Universe; that all the beings we know, from the most material molecule up to the stars circling in deepest space, obey the Laws of this Foreseeing Will, and that only Humanity is capable of reacting, destroying the harmony of the universal plan, contravening the will of heaven, and that with the sole intention of escaping the general good, and of being the only and eternally miserable creature in the whole Universe—neither logic nor metaphysics nor the ideal conception we have of God allows us to suppose this, or even to discuss it for an instant.

Besides, when we finally study the conditions of the human species, we will have an even more decisive proof of that. But let us also state, as demonstration of pure morality and just as convincing, that not a single theocratic or religious system included this frightful claim in its original dogmas. Brahmanism, Buddhism, and Christianity were all religions of love and harmony, fallen from the mouths of enlightened and benevolent apostles—only the purely human applications, political or social, have made of them instruments of terror and domination. Appropriated to the ambition of individuals, these additions are characteristic of the presumptuous earthly cooperation with the divine work; in the eyes of the sage, they have no more intrinsic value than those who have created them for personal advantages. Created by men, they have no consequences beyond Humanity.

In order not to seem emotional, we will not insist further, faced with such overwhelming proofs, where logic must corroborate our highest hopes. But let us remember that, in the very name of the Will of heaven, nothing that is contained in the Universal has the power to change the Universal in any way whatsoever.

When Humanity has risen along its curve and arrived at the

extremity of the turn that contains its modification in the Universe, it is transformed (i.e., it disappears, or in plain language, it dies). But in considering the curve of the Universe in its successive revolutions, we see immediately that there can be no disappearance there, even momentary, nor any negative phenomenon of the kind we call *death*. There is a very normal passage from one state to another, and in the operations of the Universe, this passage involves no more shocks or surprises than the passage between two consecutive moments of beings in the human cycle. There is no irregularity of any sort, either in the movement or in the Harmony: and the passage from one turn to another, or the passage of Humanity to the next modification, is only marked by a *change in the nature of the relative constitution of the beings in modification.* We will see it in a more precise, more human example, which touches us more closely, in the chapter on "The Conditions of the Individual." But one must know henceforth that the phenomenon of transmodification resides essentially and exclusively in this change alone, which is necessarily a betterment. It is an augmentation, not a diminution, and much more of a *birth* than a *death*. In reality, it is neither one nor the other, and it is as foolish to view it as an *ending*, as to call it a sudden halt, or even a derailment, when a train passes a station where the timetable does not require it to stop. These changes of modification always happen normally, carefully, and benevolently—and due to this absolute certitude, they should lose whatever they may have of temporary pain for the individual. The collectivity of beings passes from one existence to another, by diverse modalities and identical mechanisms, without there being a single instance of death, disappearance, or merely eclipse.

The divine essence that imbues the fragments of the Universe, the divine attraction that regulates their movements: these are the guarantees of their perpetuity. And Humanity, along with the whole Universe, participates in this perpetuity, at its rank of modification, and in what this modification contains of the Eternal.

Humanity, which is one of the cycles of the Universe, is not necessarily the final one. It seems very lofty to us because that is where we find ourselves, and because we understand lower cycles better than higher ones; but we are well aware of them all and convinced that we are not the beings whose relative perfection immediately precedes Total Perfection. Even in ancient mythology there are giants, demigods, and a host of intermediaries between Olympus and us; even in Christian hagiography there are Saints, Angels, and the nine celestial choirs between God and his creatures. The evident universality of opinions agrees with the dictates of feeling and the deductions of logic, to convince us that we compose one modification in the current of forms, and that we are evolving along one revolution of the indefinite cylindrical helix.

But if Humanity is not the final turn of the spiral, at least the existence of such a finality is conceivable to us. The will of Heaven, which has emitted beings into the current of forms, is the same as that which draws all beings toward itself, and consequently all must be absorbed in it. Consequently, the cylinder of creation, considered at infinity—which is precisely the metaphysical locus of Perfection—becomes a cone. And at the vertex of the cone, the helix that was rising on its lateral surface inevitably merges with it. Since the height of the cone, as we have already seen, is a geometric symbol of the attraction of the Will of Heaven, its vertex will be the metaphysical locus of the Will of Heaven itself.

We can thus consider, as a special and supreme case, the end of the last turn, namely, its meeting with the height of the cylinder and the termination of the last modification. The Chinese Sages call it the "last mechanism of transformation," and that—as logic, metaphysics, and mathematics all agree—is the re-entry of the Universe into the Will that gave it movement, and the return of all beings to the Perfection that emitted them. This return is not a "victory over contrary elements," nor is it an extraordinary transformation. Like all the other passages that preceded it, it is insensible and entirely normal. If one refers to Chapter Six, on the *Laws of Evolution*, one will see that the "transformative mechanism" changes nothing in the essence of the beings who compose the Universe; it simply entails *the ablation of Forms*, namely, the *End of the Limit*. That is what the traditional text means by saying that the "current of forms" is terminated.

In this final cycle, do we have perfect knowledge of all the preceding cycles? Do we have the stunning prescience of the final transformation? In other words, do the beings of the final cycle consider it a benefit to be deprived of their forms, or do they see it as a *death*, as we ourselves believe we see a death at the end of the human individuality? One cannot impose an opinion here, but analogy demands that the end of the final modification should cause the same impression on beings as the end of all the preceding modifications. And we have only posed this question here to emphasize, once again, how wrong it is to call the passage in question *death*, and how irrational to dread it.

This return to Total Perfection—which is determined by the *End of the Limit*, both moral and physical, that is, both the end of the current of forms and the end of the individuality of the fragments—is easy to understand through this very definition: it is the "return to the bosom of God," "Losing oneself in the Great All," "Heaven," or "Paradise." In one word that summarizes all human thought on the subject, it is *Nirvana*, or *Nibban* (which is the same word) as it is called in the Far East.

Laotseu, the greatest of the Chinese mystics, who was perhaps the world's first philosopher, defined *Nirvana* perfectly: the metaphysical locus of Active Perfection, or of the unmanifested Will of Heaven. (And, in fact, it ceases to be manifested when the current of forms is stemmed.) We will see in Laotseu's profound works how we should understand Nirvana, namely, how it is understood in the ancient texts of India, which belong to us and to all of thinking humanity. Western polemic and criticism might well have distorted it and tried to make it into something negative; modern comprehension and attacks were doing that well enough. But these incomplete scholars never dreamed that in so doing, they were complacently equating Nothingness with total activity, thus making the same gross mistake in metaphysics that the mathematical student would make, ignorantly or unconsciously, by deliberately or otherwise taking zero for the "*absence*" of a figure, or for a figure in itself, and forgetting that it is a number.

Can one conceive that beings, once absorbed in Nirvana, can issue from it anew to re-enter another current of forms, and thus to eternalize their particular movement? We have seen that mathematics replied with the necessary affirmative, because, in understanding our graphic representation, the cyclical cylinder remains a cylinder, the helix of destiny rolls eternally around its lateral surface; or the cylinder, considered at mathematical infinity, becomes a cone, and every cone presupposes another conical nappe opposed to its vertex, whose branches diverge indefinitely in the transfinite spaces. Thus, the helix is endless in both directions. But this *necessity* does not exist in metaphysics, first because metaphysical infinity, unlike mathematical infinity, does not admit any "beyond," neither in space, in volume, nor in thought; secondly because the eternity of action (willed by the manifestation of Perfection) does not invincibly demand a current of forms; the collective movement is just as much a movement as the indefinite sum of individual movements: *form* is not necessary to movement. And, lastly, the potential, nonmanifested movement is also a movement. There is no need to displace oneself to move oneself, any more than there is need to act in order to will and to think.

There is thus no necessity. But in the present state of our reasoning, we can declare that the possibility exists. For that which is possible today is possible in an indefinite manner. Only one can hardly conceive that the attraction of the will of heaven, after having reintegrated everything, disintegrates it all again. And we repeat, it is not necessary to accept this notion as if it was useful for *Eternal Activity*; movement is no more essential to *activity* than form is *essential* to being. Moreover, this is the sole point at which the Primordial Tradition remains silent, *as though it was unnecessary for the human race to have an opinion about it.* This is why two opinions exist, both acceptable: one, that the being reintegrated into Unity remains there eternally; the other, that emission into the current of forms is eternal, but that since the individual fragments are infinite in number, the same fragment does not enter twice into the current of forms (which perfectly shows how indifferent it is to the human species to choose between the two opinions).

One is therefore free to appreciate the "Transformation" or the final mechanism of the Universe as one's sentiments dictate. For all the paths chosen lead to the same unique end. And this end, happy and total Reintegration, is asserted by the written Tradition, by metaphysical and mathematical reasoning, and by the satisfaction of the three attributes that all religions essentially give to their Gods: Goodness, Justice, and Glory.

8

The Conditions of
the Individual

We have seen the nature and prospects of the Destinies of Humanity, considered as one turn on the evolutive cylinder and as one cycle in the modification of the Universe. Consequently, we know that this human cycle includes all of humanity—that is to say, the entire human species as we understand it—and all its possible varieties both before and after the present species. We have also determined the laws that invariably and inexorably control the human cycle, which is an entirely normal cycle and has nothing special about it—except for us, because we currently find ourselves there.

This natural interest that we have in the cycle wherein we are evolving, which we know a little better than the others and which we would like to know more deeply, brings us to study the movement of the human species within the cycle, and the conditions of the individual within the species.

These two studies are perfectly analogous and comprise phenomena of the same nature, all of them contingent. We will say right away that although we are leaving the domain of pure metaphysics, we will still be constrained by logic and by simple good sense to adopt, for our objective study of phenomena, only the solutions that agree with those demonstrated by the metaphysical problems. Thus, equipped with a sure and perfect guide, we approach the questions that seem the most intimate and the most obscure to the human being. At no time should we let ourselves be diverted from the path that this mental guide shows us, either by personal sensitivity, quick to fear logical solutions that seem to offend it, or by insufficient notice of the individual's inborn and unconscious egotism.

In saying that the species is to the cycle as the individual is to the species, we show by this arithmetical proportion that we can be content to study the conditions of the individual, a much easier study because it concerns us personally. Deducing general analogies will then suffice to apply it to the species: quite an easy task, which we can leave to our readers. Besides, the beginning and end of individuals, about which we are at least physically informed, give us excellent light on the beginning and end of the species. The study of the latter, framed by the experimental study of the individuals who compose it and the metaphysical study of the cycle of modifications to which it belongs, cannot have anything obscure or hazardous for our logic.

The human species is a moment of the cycle; the individual is a moment of the species. But either one can be taken as a typical unit for the purposes of study.

This typical unit obeys the four fundamental laws of the tetragram on its own level and occupies the place representing its moment on the evolutive cylinder. It should be situated immediately on the helix and on its turn, so that the design, as usual, will provide by analogy the data to be examined.

The individual under consideration is part of the species and is necessary for the constitution of the species. Its relative attributes and its essential qualities form the characteristics of the species. The one thing that does not matter is the number of individuals. We can imagine a species represented by a single individual, or by innumerable ones. Thus, one does not count the number of individuals; whatever their number, it can be more or less without modifying the species. This is what is called mathematical innumerability. And we see precisely that the individual is to the species as the point to the line, whose property is to be composed of an indefinite number of points. Thus, the graphic representation of the individual will be a point on the turn that represents its species.

If the situation of the individual on the turn is a point, its evolution with relation to the universal evolutive cylinder will be represented by a surface.*

We must add that this is not absolutely true. First, for a metaphysical reason, for if individual evolution were represented by a surface, the point of arrival would be similar to the point of departure, and thus there could be no activity (only monotony and immobility through repetition) and there would be no good, because the attraction to perfection would not be felt. Secondly, for a mathematical reason, for if evolution A were exactly a surface, it would return to its point of departure to begin evolution B, and thus the movements of the individuals would not follow the spiral turn. That is to say, the number of points that compose it would be infinite.

But this number is only indefinite, and thus evolution starting from point A on the turn comes back to point B, which is the next point, indefinitely close but mathematically distinct.

Thus, in reality, individual evolution is one turn, one function of the helix, but whose *pitch is infinitesimal.* That is why, given that we currently live, act, and reason on contingencies, we can and even must consider the diagram of this evolution as a surface. And, in reality, it possesses all the attributes and qualities of a surface, and only differs from it when considered from the Absolute. Thus, on our plane the *circulus vital* is an immediate truth, and the circle is indeed the representation of the *individual* human cycle. This brings us back to the

---

*[By "surface," the author seems to imagine the cylinder cut horizontally, hence describing a circular plane. — *Trans.*]

Western concept, which is not false, as we have been led to expect, but mistakenly applied to the movements of the Universe, whereas it should only apply to the act of man alone.

The circle of each one's individual destiny, in the Far Eastern races, is represented by the symbol of the Yin-yang:

This figure needs some brief explanations. The Yin-yang is a circle, and we have just said why. It is a circle representing evolution, individual or specific, and it only participates in two dimensions in the universal cyclical cylinder. Having no thickness, it has no opacity and is represented as diaphanous or transparent, meaning that the graphics of evolutions before or after it are visible and recorded through it.

The spiral that divides the Yin-yang circle in the form of an S is not only a symbol of the universal helix; in mathematical terms it is the *descriptive trace* of this helix itself. Let us consider the Yin-yang from the only point where it can truly be considered, that is, in relation to Perfection and "from the height of the geometrical and metaphysical locus of the will of heaven."*

One of the branches of the S-curve is the mathematical projection on the horizontal plane (descriptive geometry) of the portion of the helix that goes along the universal cylinder (becoming a cone at

---

*For explanation of this phrase, refer to the chapter on "The Laws of Evolution." [See pp. 115–29. —*Trans.*]

infinity) from the point of the turn where the Yin-yang is tangential up to reintegration in Perfection. The other branch of the S-curve is the projection (by transparency of the Yin-yang circle) of the portion of the helix that goes from active Perfection emitting forms down to the same tangential point of the turn with the Yin-yang circle. It is the whole trace of the universal curve from the will that emits it to the will that reintegrates it.

Half of the Yin-yang is black, representing evolution *below* the circle under consideration. The other half is white, which represents evolution *above* it. These two halves are equal, because since the Infinite is both point of departure and goal, in relation to the Infinite the relevant point of the turn will truly and always be at an equal distance between the point of departure and the point of arrival. The two little interior circles, one black on the white surface and the other white on the black surface, are there first to recall the "transparency" of the symbol, and then to show that these colors are not really in opposition: white exists beneath and together with the black, and black beneath and together with the white. In fact, the Yin-yang is all white, and all black, depending on whether one considers it in relation to its departure or to its goal. Moreover, for those who are deceived by mere appearances even after this explanation, it must be remembered that the Yin-yang is the symbol of individual human evolution, that is, of an activity. Hence, the symbol should be taken as active in itself, and for its proper consideration one should spin it around its center. We see then that it is *unicolored* and that, consequently, one should never presume to find there, even superficially, the slightest character of dualism.

By existing, the Yin-yang satisfies the Principle of Causality. By moving around its center with the speed of specifically human evolution, it satisfies the Law of Activity. Its circular form satisfies the Law of Harmony. By being preceded and followed by an indefinite number of concentric circles, it satisfies the Law of the Good. But let us point out—and this is grounds for profound reflection—that the three first principles are satisfied in the interior of the Yin-yang, and that satis-faction of the fourth principle (that of the Good) is found outside the Yin-yang, which means that to satisfy that principle one must consider the situation of the immediately neighboring circles. In the interior of a circle considered alone, the Law of the Good is not satisfied. In other words, *in the interior of an individual human evolution, the attraction of the will of heaven does not make itself felt.* This astonishing statement comes from the mathematical consideration of the diagram, and it will lead us to metaphysical consequences that, if not the most unexpected, are at least the most remarkable.*

Recall our demonstration that the freedom of beings does not exist, as fragments and functions of universal evolution. Absolute freedom, which contains that of contravening the designs of the will of heaven, is exclusive of this will, and of God. But we have allowed a certain freedom to the individual. Here mathematics shows us that in the vital circle of the species and the individual, the attraction of the will of heaven does not make itself felt—in other words, in the interior of its particular evolution, the individual enjoys its freedom of action. Let us consider the limits and conditions of that freedom.

The entrance into the Yin-yang and the exit from it are not at the Individual's disposal, for they are the two points that belong both to the Yin-yang and to the turn inscribed on the lateral surface of the cylinder, and which are subject to the attraction of the will of heaven. In reality, in effect, man is not free in his birth or his death. For his birth, he is not free to accept it, to refuse it, or to choose its timing. For his death, he is not free to avoid it—and in all analogous justice he should not be

---

*One should never lose sight of the fact that the Yin-yang, taken on its own, can be con-sidered as a circle, but that in the succession of individual modifications it is an element of a helix. Every individual modification is essentially a three-dimensional *vortex*. There is only one human state—and one never returns by the road one has already passed. This should cut short every more or less ingenious attempt to adapt the Primordial Tradition to pantheistic or even spiritualist theories (in the special sense that certain Western experimenters give to the latter term).

free to choose the moment of his death. Incidentally, that is why suicide is the most abnormal act, and contrary to the individual's own interests.

In any case, he is not free in any of the conditions of these two acts; birth throws him compulsorily onto the cycle of an existence that he has neither demanded nor chosen; death takes him out of this cycle and throws him compulsorily into another, prescribed and previewed by the will of heaven, which he can do nothing to modify. Thus, earthly man is a slave regarding his birth and his death, the two principal events of his individual life and the only ones that summarize his special evolution in the sight of the Infinite.

But between his birth and his death, on this two-dimensional circle, this imponderable surface of the universal volume where the attraction of the higher will is not exercised, *the individual is free.* He is absolutely free in the enactment and direction of all his earthly actions. He no longer has the will of heaven as his master—he has as guide the obscure conscience, a sort of mental instinct, which is not the same for all individuals. It evolves, becomes denser or finer with each one of them, and is in arithmetical proportion to the individual's intellectual faculties and the value of the social milieu in which he moves. It is this conscience that is the dynamic generator of his personal actions.

It is in moral phenomenalism, where this conscience serves as a mediocre instrument, that the contingencies of good and evil are born. And it is the personal belief in good and evil, each limited by the other, that makes them an objective reality in the human mind. *It is man's conscience that creates good and evil, and it is man's freedom that creates responsibilities by allowing him to follow one or the other.*

We cannot insist too much on these rational evidences—conscience, which generates good and evil, is a specific, temporary, and protean feature, even within the species. Freedom of action is extremely limited in time, and in the individual's contingencies. The acts produced by this freedom and qualified by this conscience are thus relative acts, exclusive to the species and the individual, having no value but in and through the objectivities where they are born, and indifferent in the sight of the Infinite. The merits or demerits, the benefits or offenses are of the same quality as the acts that produce them—and the sanctions attached to them by the very fact of justice, which is in the essence of the Infinite, are of the same value, the same degree, and the same repercussion as the acts that prompted them.

Man is a limited and relative being; he can only commit acts that are relative, generating relative merits, capable of relative sanctions. That which is enacted in time can only be appreciated in time: the figure drawn in a two-dimensional space cannot have three dimensions. We are hemmed in here by the axiomatic evidence of the simplest geometry. Thus, a man's act, which is a temporary and finite act, however culpable general conscience may suppose it to be, cannot bring him an eternal and infinite punishment. Hence, the eternal pains—the Hell that is not Christian, but Catholic and Roman—do not exist.

Illogical sentimentalists cry out that a fault addressed to God, an Infinite Being, deserves an infinite punishment. This is a double absurdity. A contingency cannot affect the Absolute. How then can one believe that God is so made that he can be injured by a man? It takes God to be able to offend God—and those who try to convince us of such a terrible power have never thought of that.

There is another thing. The relative freedom of man, as we have seen and demonstrated, assumes that the will of heaven exerts not attraction and is in fact indifferent to it. And in truth, man could never have acted freely if the will of heaven had not let him do so. Since it is uninterested in the matter, it cannot be offended by something in which it is uninterested, and which it does not guide, for the very reason that it has not willed to guide it.

We are not denying sanction any more than responsibility or freedom; but the limits imposed on freedom so mitigate the sanction that we see it as temporary, relative, and contingent. And now that we know it as objective on all points, we recognize it as necessary. This sanction is exercised, following the will of heaven, in the individual circle where the act was committed, or in the next circle; it does not matter, for our acts *"vibrate"* and are inscribed all along our personality in an indefinite (but not infinite) manner. And the sanction—which, like the act, is produced in time—may be postponed indefinitely along the cycles. It is thus that the product of the acts of one existence is one of the constituent elements of later existences.

But let us not forget: This purely objective element of joy or pain cannot have the least influence on the course of general evolution. Whether we have acted well or badly, the cycle that awaits us is the same for all; some traverse it in happiness, others in tears. But the class into which we rise at the end of each vital circle is the same and invincibly carries us the same distance toward the Infinite, which is our destiny.

It is a purely Taoist problem to determine the sum of our actions' vibrations and the resulting sanctions, which we will study in Kan Ying's treatise entirely devoted to it. But we have stated the principle here; as we have said, it satisfies our conscience and the idea of our freedom; it answers both the Goodness and the Justice of heaven; and it leaves intact the infrangible laws of the tradition. It puts in their proper place the contingent dualism of good and evil, and also the merits and sanctions of human actions. And it proves—so peremptorily that we will have no reason to return to it—that the belief in eternal punishments, whether held out of naivety or self-interest, is a moral barbarism, a metaphysical nonsense, and an insulting negation of the essential attributes of the Divinity.

Between birth and death, the human being is free. We have seen the reason and the means of this objective freedom, and we see its actions every day. We will also see the consequences, in the relevant part of *La Voie rationnelle*, that the West calls by the name of Morality. But phenomena apart, let us see what this birth and death are, whose timing, circumstances, and results are independent of the will of their subject.

According to all our preceding formulations and the irrefutable logic of geometry, birth is the entrance of an evolutive fragment into the human cycle, while death is the exit of this fragment from the human cycle. However, in order to enter the human cycle and to figure as an individual in that species, this fragment has to exit from the cycle inferior to the human, or to use the customary crude image, it must *die* to that cycle. Then in exiting from the human cycle, in losing the individuality of the species, the evolving fragment enters the cycle superior to the human, and in our common language it is born into this new cycle. Thus, birth and death accompany and complete one another: human birth is the immediate consequence of a death, and human death is the immediate cause of a birth. One of these circumstances never occurs without the other. And since time does not exist here, we can affirm that there is metaphysical identity between the intrinsic value of the phenomenon of birth, and the intrinsic value of the phenomenon of death. As to their relative value, and because of the immediacy of their consequences, death at the end of cycle X is superior to birth into the same cycle X, by the amount of the attraction of will of heaven on that cycle X. Mathematically, that is the value of the pitch of the evolutionary helix.* All of this may seem paradoxical, because for the sake of comprehension we are using the words *birth* and *death* to define the passages between cycles, and simple human vanity attaches a sense of increase to entry into humanity (birth) and a sense of diminution to exit from it (death), as though humanity occupied the top of a parabola, before and after which one could only descend. No error is more fatal or more ridiculous. We see metaphysically that, in the succession of cycles, *death* is an advance on *birth*, because entry into cycle X + 1 is superior to entry into cycle X. We see it geometrically on the evolutive curve of the universe. We will see it psychologically when we consider,

---

*We repeat that we do not know the essential value of this geometric element, because we have no memory of the cyclical states through which we passed and so cannot measure the metaphysical distance that separates us today from the state we came from.

in the human specimen, what elements are brought by birth, and what elements are affected by death.*

This is not the time to list the seven elements that tradition recognizes in the human species. We will see them throughout the part of these studies that concerns the physiological and psychic sciences directly derived from Laotseu's doctrine. But for now we can assert (with no surprise to those who have examined the arcana of the Hindu ternary and septenary) that the seven human elements of the Primordial Tradition can be reduced to a ternary, and that they fit very well with the ternary of *body, soul, spirit,* as the Western adepts of High Science know and define them. And it is on this ternary, familiar to all, and which even Roman Catholicism should recognize from its fundamental texts, that we will pursue our investigations and demonstration.

The human being is not an entity; it is an aggregate, and, in reality,

---

*For those who appreciate an algebraic game, we represent the data as follows: Death (*mort*) = M. Birth (*naissance*) = N. The human cycle = H. The cycle inferior to the human one = H − 1. The cycle superior to the human one = H + 1. This postulate can be applied to any cycle. Expressing the above propositions in algebraic equations, we have:

$$MH = N (H + 1), \text{ and } NH = M (H - 1)$$
$$\therefore MH = NH + N, \text{ and } NH = MH - M$$
$$\therefore MH = MH - M + N,$$
$$\therefore M = N$$

Since all coefficients and indices eliminate themselves, *the phenomena of death and birth,* considered in themselves and apart from cycles, *are perfectly equal.* Also, supposing that X is the unknown value of the improvement acquired in the course of any modification, we have:

$$M (H - 1) + NH + X = MH + N (H + 1)$$
$$\therefore MH - M + NH + X = MH + NH + N$$
$$\therefore X = M + N$$

Here, too, the coefficients eliminate each other, resulting that X (*improvement*) *is due expressly to the sum of a death and a birth* and *to the coincidence* of that death and birth. Curiously, we note that even algebraically, this X, whose substance and function we know, is *invaluable in quantity.* [Algebraic equations edited for clarity. —*Trans.*]

an aggregate of elements that are naturally not very coherent, because they differ *essentially* from one another. These three elements that make up man as we know him, exist independently from one another. There are bodies without souls or spirits, such as earthly matter; there are souls without spirits or bodies, like the invisible fluids emanated by physical, celestial, or errant forces; there are spirits without bodies, like those that Catholics call the "angelic choirs," and that correspond to an absolute reality.

We are saying nothing new here, but are presenting under a new angle the apperception of ancient things. The elements that compose man have no need to be together in order to exist, but it is their union that constitutes *man*. Before their union, humanity did not yet exist; after their dissociation, there will be no more humanity. Humanity is formed by their temporary coherence.

The phenomena of birth and death, particular to our species, therefore work not on these elements themselves, but on their assemblage and cohesion. We should even say that these elements taken individually are indifferent to birth and death, which can only affect their modalities—or their protean qualities.

This truth is already discerned and felt—if not demonstrated—for the spirit and the soul. It is no less precise in the case of matter. It would be foolish to say that the act of generation creates the matter from which the human body is formed, for the germ only fertilizes, and thereby triggers the development of the human form on condensed particles of matter. It is foolish to say that the act of death kills matter—it disintegrates it, that is, frees it from the human compound, taking away the form under which alone it could be part of man, and returns it to the current of forms, where it will not remain unutilized as long as the Universe is under the reign of the Limit.

Human birth is thus the formula for the composition of an aggregate (or, chemically, we could say the formula for the production of a precipitate). Since we are in evolution—which, speaking circumstantially, means in progress, by means of cycles, along the revolutions of the helix that leads us at the will of heaven—this birth is beneficent, in the sense that the aggregate thus formed contains superior elements to those of the preceding aggregate, whose birth into the human state has caused their immediate dissociation. The *exit* from the prehuman state corresponds to the dispersion into the universal current of an element inferior to the last human element, or of the most massive and rudimentary part of matter. The *entrance* into the human state, which coincides with it, corresponds to the acquisition of a superior element, the Spirit, or a part of the Spirit that the other state did not possess. Of course, we are always speaking in a contingent manner, because every day it becomes more scientifically probable, and more metaphysically indispensable, that the different elements of which beings are composed are different states of one and the same *Thing* (let us say, of Matter alone), purified and sublimated through individuals under the benevolent attraction of the will of heaven, by the continual efforts of the personality.

The phenomenon of death is absolutely identical. Its analogous effects appear to us in reverse only because we have acquired the bad habit of considering it from the sole point of view of the human state. The *exit* from this state (death) corresponds to the dissolution of the body, to loss of the human material form, which is the lowest part of our compound. But entrance into the suprahuman state (birth) that coincides with human death brings the accession of a spiritual element whose value we do not know, and which is superior to the best of our human elements. That is why human death, since it coincides with a better birth, is metaphysically superior to human birth.

Here, then, the human aggregate is rightly defined. None of its elements belong to it alone, because they are all parts of other aggregates, whether lower or higher. None of them is essentially affected by human phenomena. The aggregate is made solely by the temporary association of these independent elements. What characterizes the human being is that nowhere else are these elements found assembled, in the order and with the coefficients that they have in our state. The human specificity is not one of essence, nor of nature; it is a specificity of degree and method. This degree, this method—in a word, this particular *arrangement*—is the INDIVIDUAL.

But that is not all there is to man. Here we touch the metaphysical depth of what concerns our present state. The elements of the human aggregate, which we have agreed to condense into three principal ones, are independent of one another. In the evolution of the Universe, they carry different and even disparate qualities, whose interplay tends to distance them from one another, as we have already determined above. Yet the human aggregate, if not as homogenous as one might wish, is solid—it possesses an *interior* force of cohesion that it obeys.

It has been said that this force of cohesion was the divine will. That may be so; the said force is evidently a consequence of the divine will. But it is not the will of heaven itself. If we go back to the unarguable geometrical conceptions of previous chapters, we will see that the will of heaven is not felt in the human state. It is precisely because of this that man possesses a relative freedom, and that the graphic symbol of his state can be a circle and not a helical revolution. This force is not the will of Heaven, nor is it the force of the elements constituting humanity, which is a personal force, independent and consequently centrifugal in relation to the human compound.

This *force*, which is an emanation of the will of heaven, belongs exclusively to us. This force that *holds together* the human aggregate, and *which gives birth to and animates the individual*, is the PERSONALITY.

Individuality and Personality: These are different states that are not on the same plane. They have nothing of the same organization or the same existence, and of which the second is superior to the first with all the superiority of eternity over time. An unfortunate habit has made these terms synonymous, or at least analogous, and their confusion has created deplorable errors in scientific arguments and in the popular imagination. When we know that the person is the source of all the successive individuals who have represented the cohesive force mentioned above, we will understand how propositions and whole systems harmonize and cohere, though they seemed adverse due to a faulty definition or a confusion of objects.

The *individuality* appears to be the personality considered in one cycle. In reality, it is not even that, for the personality exists in its entirety outside the individual and is affected neither by its birth nor by its death, nor by any of its changes within the cycle. To be precise, the individuality is the result of the effort of the personality on a compound, such as a human compound. Consequently, the individuality is absolutely bound to the compound and is transformed with it, whereas the personality subsists, always self-identical.

Thus, the human individual, who is the result of the physiological and psychological influences of the elements of the human compound on one another, appears, develops, and disappears at the same time as the compound of which it is the expression. The personality is called the human personality as long as it is working on the compound, but that is only an avatar, a temporary measure of its value. Today it applies itself to the human compound, yesterday to the compound that preceded it, tomorrow to the compound that follows—and it is always self-similar, because the nature and the determinants of a force are independent of its point of application. The individual is thus protean and contingent, whereas the personality is immortal and contains the indefinite succession of individuals.

We can now see clearly what constitutes the "human personality," a particle of the universal personality. It is made from a human aggregate, which constitutes the individual; also from the movements that the individual's elements generate between themselves through their proximity. Finally, it is composed of the movements that the personality imprints, in its effort of cohesion over the individual.

By an acceptable analogy, one can infer that the first term of this human trinity corresponds to the body, the second to the soul, the third to the spirit—not, of course, in their essence but in their manifestation. But it would be wrong to press too far the consequences of this analogy, which was made for the sake of simplification, and then not to create new categories.

Here the Buddhist and Pythagorean Law of Rebirths, misinterpreted even by many of its adepts, is explained, proven, and avenged of all its injuries. It must not be understood to refer to individuals, because it is contrary to their condition—it must refer to the personality, which when one individual (i.e., a field of action and effort) disappears, takes over another individual: meaning that when an individual *dies*, it is *reborn* in another individual. We note that the choice of individual is such as always to satisfy the four primordial Laws of Activity, Liberty, Harmony, and the Good. Here, too, *animal* metempsychosis would appear as absurd nonsense and a true barbarity. Thus, the personality—which at a given moment was, is, or will be the human personality, following the momentum of the cycles under consideration—will go from one existence to another until *"the reintegration in the supreme existence, in God."* There is no better place to demonstrate that when there is agreement about definitions, there is only one way to say the truth. Nor is there a better place for this phrase, intentionally italicized, from an occultist who was exclusively Western: my dear friend and brother Stanislas de Guaita.

Our vague desire for the infinite is satisfied by this immutability of the personality. It is here that one should place the much more precise affection that we have for ourselves, through our companions. It will suffice us, if we can sublimize these affections and detach ourselves from the lower aspirations, which are too heavy to follow us in the indefinite ascent of the evolutive helix. It is this that Christianity calls the immortality of the soul. It is both the witness and the promise of our eternity.

This distinction—so profound, so necessary, and which seems

subtle only because it has been so long misunderstood—explains to us the Law of Rebirths, of which we can all be devotees whatever our traditional cult. It also explains the rational phenomenon of human death, and the cause of the tragic heartbreak and horror that it inspires in us.

We have amply demonstrated how every *death* (and human death is no exception) is a beneficent passage from any given state to a higher one. Hence, the deepest thinkers have aspired toward death as being the only means for their perfecting. But at the moment of transition all humans, including these thinkers, rebel with all their being. Despite all our metaphysical rationales, when we see one of own die before us, we are seized with terror and sorrow. We weep both for the departed and for ourselves who will follow him. How can we explain this universal emotion, which would be insane if other factors than those we have just shown did not enter into play?

It is because we are particularly affected by the elements that this passage most touches and disturbs. Let us consider psychically the role of human death in the evolution of our personality.

The body, which is the characteristic form of the species, has no further reason to exist, and in fact it *disappears* more or less rapidly, to take on other shapes. It becomes another form, as indifferent to us as any inanimate human form. The stupor and the cause of sorrow does not lie there.

The personality, as we have seen, subsists, augmented and perfected by the existences that it has traversed and the individualities it has animated. It is augmented through its own effort, which the individuality wherein it has been working yields up to it at the moment of its separation. And this baggage that the personality carries with itself into other cycles is the sacred heritage of our ideas, our concepts, our labors, and our sufferings. And since the personality rises by one degree in order to individualize anew, that is not where regret lies.

But we have shown that the human compound also contained the movements caused by the coexistence of its elements, and by the sum of its elements vis à vis its personality.

These are not its ideas, which are the daughters of its personality and of the will of heaven. They are its impressions, its affections—in a word, its *human emotions.* Will the personality take them with it? No, because they were human. Will we find them again someday? Feel them similarly elsewhere? No. For that it would be necessary to recover all the elements that made up these impressions, all the elements of the human compound associated in the same fashion and with the same coefficients; in other words, one would have to find the characteristics of the human cycle in another cycle. That is what is impossible. Certain human elements will be found, but never all of them, nor of the same value; they will not influence each other in the same way, and the personality will no longer impose on them with the same results. The *"Emotions of man"* are thus specific to man and vanish with him. And while his body returns to matter to enter into another current of forms, and his unalterable spirit leads the personality in its ascent, his *soul*—which is the most tenuous of materials, but which is still matter, as even the princes of the Catholic church admit*—dissolves into the psychic world, in the ether of vibrations, in the domain of wandering forces about which we still know so little, but whose reduced energy is known today to be *literally astral.* That which was man's psychic characteristic, we will never find again.

We cannot rationally regret it, because its disappearance is immediately replaced by an element of analogous essence and superior quality. But we prefer impulsively what we have and know to that which we do not know. We are attached to this bundle of impressions and sentiments, all the more since it is the characteristic of our human state. This exclusively human sensibility, the emotional cord that joins us to

---

Anima: materia prima (St. Thomas Aquinas, Q. 75 [*Summa Theologiae*]); cf. also Pope Clement V's bull on the same subject.

others, was what we held most dear. And it is that alone which merges into the universal, with no possible return to individualization!

Note, too, that this suffering is all the more grievious to us because the location of suffering from the loss of this element is precisely in the element itself. It is not with our sensuality, nor with our reason, but with our emotion that we mourn the departure of the emotional sum represented by the person who dies beside us. And this is so true that our most bitter regrets go not to the man of genius, who held us by the brain, nor to our parents who held us by blood, but to those whose life was parallel to our own, whose actions were kindred to our own actions and, consequently, whose emotions penetrated our own and very often determined their movements.

Few can claim immunity to this irrational yet natural grief, which is from *human altruism*, that is, *generalized egotism*, because reason itself is impotent against it. And the indulgences of our emotions are only mastered by the most powerful will. But that is not the point. Let us be content to have analyzed death, and to have precisely dissected it, to the point of the very emotions that it arouses in us.

Having said what birth is and what human life is, we cannot yet leave the study of the final condition of the individual. For as we have already said, the eternal personality engraves the evolutive helix, laden after its fashion with the sublimized sum of known ideas and received impressions. Thus, even that which concerns the emotional human state does not perish altogether. No more do the preceding states perish. Our personality, individualized with the appropriate motions of the human state, is the heritage of former cycles of which we are unconscious. We cannot deny them just because we have no memory of them. We have a clear appetence for the future, and obscure memories of the past, like veiled flashes: appetence and vague memories that are appropriate to our human state. It is logical that while rising through the cycles, knowledge of the future and memory of the past should illuminate our intelligence. And then we will conceive as axiomatic these profound truths, which today we can only hope to glimpse through analogies.

Let us realize, then, that the passage in the human state profits us not only for our evolution but for the definitive formation of our entity, and that the best awaits us through these rebirths whose ancient law we have just corroborated. Let us realize that nothing we do, say, or think is absolutely lost. Even that emotionality that makes us wrongly consider departure from the earthly state as the worst of evils finds its full satisfaction in the end. As we conclude quite a rigorous study, may we be excused for this digression into the emotional domain. Our only intention is to prove thereby the excellence of traditional logic, and the prescient omnipotence of the Will of heaven.

Since the goal of Evolution is unity, all the sentiments aroused by physical beauties, all the ideas aroused by emotional beauties, inscribed in the sequence of modifications, point toward the metaphysical place where all beauties, turned to splendor, and all ideas, turned to Truth, vanish consciously in Perfection.

Thus, in the course of cycles, the personalities who approach each other through such individualizations become closer at every moment. These earthly unions, whatever we call them, that we fear will be dissolved by death, are re-knitted through the modifications, to the degree that our elements are perfected. Close as human ties may seem to us, we are further from one another today than we will ever be in future cycles. Our harsh and severe logic thus leads us to an inevitable result that satisfies emotion, relieved of course from its native egotism, better than all our reveries and fantasies. The affinities that we find in the human milieu are the result of efforts in other cycles preceding our own; they are likewise the preparation and the promise of closer and more disinterested ties between the very beings who formed them and will become modes of their personality. Thus, the pure ideas, those who conceived them, those who stimulated them, and those who adored themselves in them, are all sublimized and raised by the current of benevolent Evolution, as we rise together *eternally reunited* into the Universal.*

Here we shall end this summary of the *Metaphysical Way* as followed and guarded by the Far Eastern Tradition, which—pending other discoveries—is the only Tradition to have been preserved up to our time without interpolation, suppression, or obscuration. We would have made it shorter if we had not feared making the comprehension of these delicate matters still more obscure. Further studies in the same spirit will treat the philosophy of Laotseu, as *The Rational Way*, and that of Kongtzeu (Confucius) as *The Social Way*, both of them narrowly and directly derived from the same Tradition.

In conclusion, we would like to leave a practical corollary to the metaphysical outline that we have sketched, by extracting from it a compatible and practical working method for those who are curious not only to read the preceding text, but to undertake the task that it invites and recommends.

This working method is deduced logically from the principles that we have established. We will explain it in a few words.

The active destiny of man breaks forth in the activity afforded him by the cyclical modification of which current humanity is a part. We are not the masters of this activity, nor of its goal or even of its

---

*It will be noticed in this metaphysical study that we have treated the human state by considering it apart from all the other states. What we have said about it can be generally applied to every other specific state, every other individual vortex. We merely repeat that the individual passes only once through the same species, and that its vortex is only the application to its individuality of the figurative turn of the evolution of the species. As for the relations of the vortices to each other and to states between them, the Chinese Tradition treats their study in another part of its philosophy. In fact, the succession of states has something regular and coordinated about it, which is in the domain of Reason. The modifications that emanate from the being, the transformation that reintegrates beings, and the Nirvana (*Nibban*) that is the crown and the end of the series, should be studied in their reciprocal movements and influences. Wenwang's own text says it expressly: "Modification and transformation, that is the *Rational Way* of activity." Hence, we will find it explained in the *Philosophy of the Rational Way*, namely, in the Taoist system of Laotseu.

means. But in order to obey the will of heaven, we should conform our movement to its own, and also, as Tsheou Kong expressly says, silence the human desires that hinder the good result of this activity. How could this personal and cerebral movement of the human being be better employed than in studying the activity of heaven, which is our model—especially since such a study enables us to participate as far as possible in that activity?

The activity of Heaven causes everything to modify and transform; hence, its study can never be complete. Scarcely has it been expressed than it is no longer exact, even if it could have been at that precise moment. Thus, the study of heaven is never finished; it is even never begun. Yet we should not fear to dedicate all our reasoning efforts to it.

How is this study to be done? It must be done with the goal of acting in parallel and beneath the activity of heaven. Such is the corollary of the great symbolic formula: with all principles, all freedom, all harmony, all good. "With all principles" means relying on the principle of the activity of heaven and on those that flow from it. "With all freedom" means disengaging oneself from all passions, which chain us down. "With all harmony" means deducing all the consequences from all the principles in a logical and regular way. "With all good" means following the rule of perfectible reason that comes to us from Heaven. Under these conditions, the work of the gifted man will be favorable to him. Besides, in this study there is no error for which heaven can entirely blame us. Any responsibility we might have would go back beyond the present moment; errors are not blamed on us if they do not arise from our immediate will. So long as we observe in our studies the principles according to which heaven moves, our errors are only due to the relative imperfection of our present modification.

At such a height every conception, even false, even crazy, has merit and does homage. Insufficient ideas, detestable terms: that is what makes up our studies because of our nature and the mediocrity of our means. Does that mean that we should give up on them, and content ourselves with the faith of infants and simpletons? Assuredly not. Intelligence abandoned by man, of which he can only boast if he uses it, makes him guilty of immobility; it will be counted against him as indifference. Alternatively, we may fear that in searching for the truth we will only find error and become attached to it, and then lose confidence in heaven and in the destiny it has conferred on us. The fearless vision of that which is above us is the duty of the modification of our spirit, in order for it to attain its definitive transformation.

There are no errors for this center, which is One and All. In facing the Essence, there is no appreciable divergence between two contrary affirmations pronounced by us, nor between what we call the true and the false. Human truth and falsity are so far distant from the Truth that, considered in relation to it, they blend at infinity in one and the same inexactitude. Such error is meritorious when we commit it with an ardent and pure heart, following the Way of Heaven.

Whichever path one takes, one is always inevitably moving toward the Center. Every step taken by our studies, in any direction, brings us closer to it. The concepts, naturally false, that we enunciate today vibrate in our whole personality and beyond the limits that our senses impose on the present world. In rising from turn to turn, through the modifications that await us, they are divested of error, at the same time as they throw off the ridiculous terms with which we have necessarily clothed them.

All work, all thought, even all dreams are thus propitious. We should not fear missteps and troubles for which we are only responsible due to our present nature and destiny. And it is only by accumulating errors that the gifted man will one day attain the summit of the Truth.

9

The Instruments
of Divination
Texts and Documents

It seems appropriate to give some texts and documents extracted from the *Yiking* and from various commentaries or philosophical paraphrases of the maxims of Fohi and Wenwang. We have seen that the *Yiking* addressed all conditions of human existence, all the contingent sciences, and the very study of metaphysics and the subjective. It also had a divinatory meaning. Along with political symbolism, this is certainly the most popular part of the primordial text.

Admittedly, it is also the worst interpreted and the least understood. The sages and philosophers of the Far East were never interested in empiricism and never applied their favorite studies to the divinatory aspect of the *Yiking*. Only the wandering priests called *taosse*, and who rightly or wrongly occupied a station between mendicant monks and jugglers, made this study their passion, beside making their living from it. Left to the mercies of mediocre minds, the divinatory tradition of the *Yiking* was soon obscured, and one may say that nowadays it is completely lost.

We are not going to have the naive audacity even to try to reconstitute it, for the texts of the Book are almost unintelligible without the Oral Tradition, or at least their sense of it is so vague that one can draw from them any interpretation one likes. It must be admitted that the divinatory Oral Tradition has been defunct for centuries—and we can even be precise in saying for twenty-one centuries.

Laotseu and Confucius knew it; Laotseu disdained it as an inferior game. Confucius transmitted it to his disciples, but one finds no trace of it since the destruction of the Books and the execution of the Learned, ordered by Emperor Thsinchi-Hoang-ti (213 BCE).

Our care for exactitude leads us to confess that we have nowhere met with written explanations or authorized commentators on divination. If any exist, they are hidden in the depths of the last sanctuaries, or else they guard their trust so jealously that even the Far Eastern initiates of high grade do not suspect their existence.

This was also the opinion of Monsieur Philastre, from whom I borrow passages from his excellent translation of the *Yiking*, on which I cannot improve. Under these conditions, it is no surprise that we are presenting almost incomprehensible texts and almost undecipherable diagrams; but it is still useful for these texts and diagrams not to disappear entirely from human memory. Perhaps some kabbalist or scholar, profoundly versed in Western sciences, will be able to find points of resemblance and common traits with divination systems such as Greece and the Middle Ages have transmitted to us. In any case, we do not think that light can be shed on it from the Far East, where Philastre has been forced to admit himself lost in darkness.

We have chosen Philastre's translations in places where we have not been obliged to translate the text for the first time. Philastre was not only an outstanding sociologist, the like of whom was never seen in the halls of our various Institutes. He spent much of his life in China and Indochina: as a worthy officer of the Marine, an expert and distinguished philosopher, he profited by his long stay among the Far Easterners to enter into their minds, their tradition, and their society. Thanks to his high culture and a rare talent for assimilation, he overcame the resistance of the prudent mandarins of the Empire, and crossed thresholds that are usually closed, and almost never open to men of another race. Thus, he received the most valuable teachings, and at the same time as certain serious advantages, received instructions and cooperated with interlocutors who enabled his translation of the "Primordial Tradition" to be the best monument one could ever expect to erect in a Western language in honor of the Chinese philosophies.

These advantages would have gone nowhere without his duties toward the race that had welcomed him, and the sages who had elevated his mind.

In the Far East these duties took on a particularly serious and coercive form. Philastre realized it too late, when after the death of the heroic Garnier at Tonkin, he accepted the mission to treat with the empire of Annam as plenipotentiary, in the name of France. The obligations of his heart were in contradiction with those of his commission; he tried in vain to reconcile them and was the victim of an inextricable situation. Moved by a spirit of veneration and obedience to his masters, he tried to conclude a treaty that would not disadvantage them. Thus, he seemed to ignore the interests of his own country, and at the same time, despite all, he betrayed the most secret desires of his conscience. He was relieved of his functions, left the Far East without the slightest thought of returning, and had to be content with a low-grade teaching position in the South of France, where he died poor and unknown, having gained from all his work and knowledge only the constancy of his resignation.

I wanted to highlight these few traces of a truly tragic existence, so as to draw this lesson from it: that to engage oneself in an intellectual impasse leads to the social ruin of the individual.

THE NUMBERS

A. Heaven is one, three, five, seven, nine. Earth is two, four, six, eight, ten. These are the numbers of heaven and earth. The numbers 1 and 6 are situated at the bottom; 2 and 7, at the top; 3 and 8, on the left; 4 and 9, on the right; 5 and 10, in the middle.

B. The number five indicates the extension of that which engenders; the number ten, the extension of that which is engendered. One, two, three, and four represent the situation of the four symbols; six, seven, eight, and nine are the numbers that correspond to them.

C. There are five heavenly numbers, and five earthly numbers: in each series the numbers concord, two by two. The sum of the first is 25; the sum of the second is 30; their total is 55. This is what accomplishes the states of expansion and contraction. The heavenly numbers are odd; the earthly numbers, even. 1 and 2, 3 and 4, 5 and 6, 7 and 8, 9 and 10, form concordant groups. Equally, in the five situations, two corresponding numbers concord, namely: 1 and 6, 2 and 7, 3 and 8, 4 and 9, 5 and 10. Unity is modified and engenders water; 6 transforms it. 2 engenders fire; 7 transforms it. 3 engenders wood; 8 transforms it. 4 engenders gold; 9 transforms it. 5 modifies earth; 10 transforms it. Thus, the five agents and the five planets undergo the phenomena of contraction and rectification, going and returning.

D. After the *secret center* of the *river diagram*, the heavenly number five multiplies the earthly number, making 50. But when one consults the lot by means of this number, one limits the use to 49.

ON THE MANNER OF OPERATING DIVINATION BY THE USE OF *SHI* GRASS

Suspend *one* between the little finger of the left hand and the next finger. Separate what remains after having counted off the stalks by fours. Collect in the two gaps flanking the middle finger of the left hand. As soon as the operation is finished, pick up all; reunite and separate as before, so as to group them in two hands, and thus repeat the same operation.

E. The lots relating to positivity are 216, those relating to negativity are 144, making 360 in all, equal to the days of one revolution.

F. The *river diagram* with four faces: the great positivity is 1, and is followed by the number 9; the little positivity is 3, followed by 6; the little negativity is 2, followed by 8. The rule for counting and eliminating the stalks (stalks of *shi* grass, which represent in divination the lines of the hexagrams) consists of adding what remains after the three modifications, taking away unity from the beginning, and counting each group of 8 as a duality. Unity is surrounded in a circle by 3; duality is enclosed in a square by 4; 3 uses the totality; 4 uses division. By reuniting all, it gives the numbers 6, 7, 8, 9, and after three eliminations everything will be reunited. Three extra unities remain, which repeated thrice give 9. Thus, there are 4×9 stalks $= 36$, a number that constitutes the extreme positivity $= 1$. $36 = 3 + 6 = 9$; $9 + 1 = 10$.

If, on the contrary, three dualities are left, that makes 6, and the number of stalks will be $4 \times 6 = 24$, which constitutes extreme negativity—4. $24 = 2 + 4 = 6$; $6 + 4 = 10$. Such is the mystery of transformation; the purpose of this is exclusively to show the formation of numbers.

The hexagrams contain 192 positive lines and as many negatives. Now $192 \times 36 = 6,912$, and $192 \times 24 = 4,608$, making in all 11,520 formulas of divinations. Perform the four operations: division into two groups, suspension of one stalk, elimination by fours, gathering of the remainder. Three modifications determine one formula; eighteen determine a hexagram.

The six lines being complete, considering some as movement, the others as rest, it follows that a single hexagram can become successively any of the sixty-four lines, and serve to determine the predictions. These modifications present 4,096 different lots: $4,096 = 64^2$.

All these questions were completed and developed in the lost instructions of Tcheouli to the functionaries charged with divination, but it is absolutely impossible to verify them today.*

THE TESTS

A. Man asks a question; by means of the signs, he receives a reply. As from an echo, he receives the order that prescribes his destiny. There is nothing distant from him, nothing obscure or hidden. He has knowledge and awareness of the beings who are arriving.

B. After having counted three by three for the modification, one again counts five by five: one seeks the numbers seven, eight, nine, ten, to determine the symbol of movement or repose. One must scrutinize the analogies and differences in the words so as to know the distinctions between the members of the groups; then comes the test by three and by five, so as to compare the beings and the words. (These two texts are extracts from the works of Weifei.)

THE SIGNS

A. The Yi includes the extreme origin, which is where the two rules are born: the two engender the four symbols, which engender the eight trigrams. Thus, the order is always well traced, when it is a matter of divination.

B. The instruments of divination are stalks of grass and the tortoise; by them, one determines the fortunate or unfortunate presages of the universe. Heaven shows the symbols; the sage deduces the presages from them. The diagram comes out of the river, the book out of the lake, and the saint formulates the

---

*Paragraphs A, C, and E are translated from the determinative formulae of Wenwang and Tscheou Kong; paragraph B from the commentary of Tsheng-tse; and paragraphs D and F from the work of Tsouhi titled *The Dissipation of Darkness.*

rules from them. The formulas annexed to the symbols serve to determine the warning.

C. The fortunate or unfortunate presages are always the result of destiny traced by the formulas; it is by the movement of the modifications that these presages become evident. Fohi saw the symbols in the sky and the formulas on the ground. Two eyes exchange glances; beings exist.

D. Fohi made knots in string for hunting and fishing. He took that from the trigram Li. Shennong bent wood to make a plow; he took that from the trigram Yi. He founded the market so that men from the whole universe could make their exchanges there; he took that from the trigram She ho.

Hoan ghi, Yao, and Shouen shi governed; they directed the people so that they would not be idle; they enlightened them so that the people would conform to the Good; they took that from the two trigrams of Perfection. They split a tree to make a canoe, they cut wood to make an oar; they took that from the trigram Hoan. They harnessed oxen for transport; they mounted horses; they took that from the trigram Souei. They doubled the gates to receive dangerous guests; they took that from the trigram Yu. They took a tree to make a pestle and scooped out the ground to make a mortar; they took that from the trigram Siae Kio. They bent and cut wood to make a bow and arrows; they took that from the trigram Kouei. They raised columns and sloped forms to construct houses; they took that from the trigram Tatsheng. They made use of inner and outer coffins; they took that from the trigram Tae Kouo. They invented the characters of writing, and tablets; they took that from the trigram Koue.*

---

*Paragraphs B and D are translated from the formulae of Wenwang and Tsheou Kong; paragraph A from the *Kimong* of Tsouhi; and paragraph C from the same author's commentary.

THE CONCORDANCES

In olden times, the holy man secretly perceived the mysterious causes of light and created divination. He tripled heaven, doubled earth, and relied on numbers; he exhausted the reason of being and completely embraced the nature of man, so as to attain to destiny. Heaven and earth determined the situations; the mountain and the marsh freely blended their ethers; lightning and wind entered into contact, water and fire did not destroy one another. To know what has passed conforms to the common way; to know what is to come is above the common way.

Lightning shakes; wind scatters; rain soaks; the sun evaporates; the obstacle blocks; satisfaction rejoices; heaven governs; passivity embraces.

The supreme being results from movement; it equals itself in the universe; it sees itself in transformation; it acts in passivity; it speaks in satisfaction; it fights in activity; it endeavors in displacement; it ends its word in the final halt.*

Movement, which is the Dragon: here is the mysterious cause of all beings.

Khien, activity; khouen, passivity; tshen, movement; souen, entrance; khan, fall; li, vibration, ken, stop; touei, satisfaction.

Khien, horse; khouen, mare; tshen, Dragon; souen, hen; khan, pig; li, pheasant; ken, fox; touei, ram. Examples taken at a distance. Khien,

---

*These concordances require the graphic explanation of the eight primitive trigrams:

three continuous lines, ☰ Khien, ☰ heaven;
one continuous between two broken lines, ☵ Khan, ☵ water;
a broken line above two continuous lines, ☱ touei, ☱ swamp;
a broken line below two continuous lines, ☴ souen, ☴ wind;
a broken line between two continuous lines, ☲ li, ☲ fire;
a continuous line above two broken lines, ☶ ken, ☶ mountain;
a continuous line under two broken lines, ☳ tshen, ☳ lightning;
three broken lines, ☷ Khouen, ☷ earth.

head; khouen, belly; tshen, feet; souen, thigh; khan, ear; li, eye; ken, hand; touei, mouth. Examples taken on the body. Khien, heaven, is the father; khouen, earth, is the mother; tshen, male principle; souen, female principle; khan, husband; li, wife; ken, boy; touei, girl.

Khien: that is the sun, that which is round, the precious stone, the prince, gold, cold, ice, red, the fast horse, the white horse, the dry tree, that which is straight, clothing, the word.

Khouen: that is the earth, fabric, the ax, economy, equality, the mother of the bull, the chariot, appearance, the crowd, the tool-handle, black, that which is square, darkness, the sack, the pipe, the fly.

Tshen: that is the Dragon, lightning, yellow, the causative influence, the great road, the elder son, haste, bamboo, harmonious song, the mane, the return to life, repetition, the crow.

Souen: that is wood, wind, the elder daughter, the weft, white, labor, length, elevation, the branch, the sense of smell, the broad brow, benefice, the tree, the search.

Khan: that is water, the hidden secret, the roof, the bowstring, illness, the revolution of the blood, pale red, ardor, the fine foot, the cover, calamity, the moon, the robber, hardness of heart, the cave, music, the spiny thicket, the fox.

Li: that is fire, the sun, lightning, the girl, posterity, the weapon, the tortoise, the belly, the reptile, the fruit, the branch, the cow.

Ken: that is the mountain, the path, the stone, the gate, the monk, the finger, the mouse, solitude, the nose, the tiger, the wolf.

Touei: that is the marsh, the child, the soothsayer, the tongue, the rupture, duration, the concubine, the ram, permanence.*

Note: One may conclude from the preceding texts:

1. That divination was in fact determined by Wenwang and Tsheou Kong.

---

*This entire text is excerpted from Chapter VI of the "Ten Wing-beats" of Kongtzeu (Confucius).

2. That the rules of divination lie in the science of numbers, and that counting is done with stalks of *shi* grass.

3. That the manipulation of stalks of *shi* grass led to the examination of one of the sixty-four hexagrams.

4. That this examination should be done by taking as mental director one of the hexagrammatic positions, following the formula of the question. Thus, there were sixty-four ways of doing the examination of the hexagram indicated by the manipulation and, consequently, there were 64^2 or 4,096 ways of replying to a question.

5. Finally, that following the question, the meaning of each of the trigrams composing the hexagrams was indicated in the concordances.

One can find other things analogically in the preceding texts. But the state of the tradition, solely from the divinatory viewpoint, does not allow us to judge whether what one can find in these texts is really what their writers wanted one to find there.

Index

Page numbers in *italics* refer to illustrations.